So
Coach

Solution Focused Coaching in Practice is a practical 'how-to' guide that provides an invaluable overview of Solution Focused Coaching skills and techniques.

Reflecting upon published research on the solution focused approach, Bill O'Connell, Stephen Palmer and Helen Williams bring their own experiences of Solution Focused Coaching together with others in the field to cover topics such as:

- the coach–coachee relationship
- the role of technology in coaching
- inclusive coaching
- group and team coaching
- practical issues and skills.

Incorporating coachee case studies, worksheets, practice tips and discussion points, the skills, strategies and techniques in this book are straightforward to apply and can be used in most coaching settings. This practical book is essential reading for experienced personal or executive coaches, managers considering introducing a new and better coaching culture for their staff, and for those just starting out on their coaching journey.

Bill O'Connell is Director of Training at Focus on Solutions and a Fellow of the British Association of Counselling and Psychotherapy.

Stephen Palmer is Honorary Professor of Psychology at City University and Director of its Coaching Psychology Unit, UK. He is Founder Director of the Centre for Coaching, London, UK.

Helen Williams is a coaching psychologist and associate consultant at the Centre for Coaching, London. She is a faculty member of the International Academy for Professional Development, London, UK.

Essential Coaching Skills and Knowledge
Series Editors: Gladeana Mcmahon,
Stephen Palmer and Averil Leimon

The **Essential Coaching Skills and Knowledge** series provides an accessible and lively introduction to key areas in the developing field of coaching. Each title in the series is written by leading coaches with extensive experience and has a strong practical emphasis, including illustrative vignettes, summary boxes, exercises and activities. Assuming no prior knowledge, these books will appeal to professionals in business, management, human resources, psychology, counselling and psychotherapy, as well as students and tutors of coaching and coaching psychology.

www.routledgementalhealth.com/essential-coaching-skills

Titles in the series:

Cognitive Behavioural Coaching in Practice: An Evidence Based Approach
Edited by Michael Neenan and Stephen Palmer

Brief Coaching: A Solution Focused Approach
Chris Iveson, Evan George and Harvey Ratner

Solution Focused Coaching in Practice

Bill O'Connell, Stephen Palmer and Helen Williams

Routledge
Taylor & Francis Group
LONDON AND NEW YORK

First published 2012
by Routledge
27 Church Road, Hove, East Sussex BN3 2FA

Simultaneously published in the USA and Canada
by Routledge
711 Third Avenue, New York NY 10017

Routledge is an imprint of the Taylor & Francis Group, an informa business

British Library Cataloguing in Publication Data
A catalogue record for this book is available from the British Library

Library of Congress Cataloging-in-Publication Data
O'Connell, Bill, 1946–
Solution focused coaching in practice / Bill O'Connell, Stephen Palmer, Helen Williams.
    p. cm.—(The essential coaching skills and knowledge)
  Includes bibliographical references and index.
  1. Employees—Coaching of.   2. Executive coaching.   3. Personal coaching.
  4. Solution-focused therapy.   I. Palmer, Stephen, 1955–   II. Williams, Helen,
  1975–   III. Title.
  HF5549.5.C53O36 2012
  658.3'124—dc23

                                                                    2011052603

ISBN: 978-0-415-44706-5 (hbk)
ISBN: 978-0-415-44707-2 (pbk)
ISBN: 978-0-203-11173-4 (ebk)

Typeset in Century Schoolbook MT
by RefineCatch Limited, Bungay, Suffolk, UK

MIX
Paper from
responsible sources
FSC
www.fsc.org   **FSC® C004839**   Printed and bound by CPI Group (UK) Ltd, Croydon, CR0 4YY

Dedications

For Ella, Clara and George, whose grandpa I am honoured to be, wishing you solutions for the next generation (BO'C)

For my mother, Cecila Palmer (SP)

For my husband Ben and son Ry, and for my Mum, Dad and sisters Lisa and Lorna, with love and thanks for making this possible (HW)

Contents

Illustrations

Tables

Figures

About the authors

Bill O'Connell is the Director of Training at Focus on Solutions, an independent training agency specialising in Solution Focused training. He was formerly the Programme Leader for the Masters programme at Birmingham University and is a Fellow and a Senior Accredited Counsellor of BACP. He has written extensively on the Solution Focused approach, and is the author of *Solution Focused Therapy* (1998/2005) and *Solution Focused Stress Counselling* (2001). He co-edited *The Handbook of Solution Focused Therapy* (2003) with Professor Stephen Palmer. When he's not working Bill enjoys looking after and having fun with his grandchildren, playing golf enthusiastically but badly, and supporting Glasgow Celtic. Bill can be contacted at bill@focusonsolutions.co.uk and through www.focuson-solutions.co.uk.

Stephen Palmer PhD is Founder Director of the Centre for Coaching, London UK and Managing Director of the International Academy for Professional Development Ltd. He is an Honorary Professor of Psychology at City University London and Founder Director of their Coaching Psychology Unit. He is Honorary President of the International Society for Coaching Psychology, was the first Honorary President of the Association for Coaching, and the first Chair of the British Psychological Society Special Group in Coaching Psychology. He is the UK Coordinating Co-Editor of the *International Coaching Psychology Review*, and Executive Editor of *Coaching: An International Journal of Theory,*

Research and Practice. He has authored or edited over 35 books including *The Handbook of Solution Focused Therapy* (with O'Connell, 2003), the *Handbook of Coaching Psychology* (with Whybrow, 2007), *The Coaching Relationship: Putting People First* (with McDowall, 2010), *Developmental Coaching: Life Transitions and Generational Perspectives* (with Panchal, 2011) and *Cognitive Behavioural Coaching in Practice: An Evidence Based Approach* (with Neenan, 2012). In 2008 the British Psychological Society, Special Group in Coaching Psychology gave him the 'Lifetime Achievement Award in recognition of distinguished contribution to coaching psychology'.

Helen Williams is a qualified coaching psychologist and Associate Consultant at the Centre for Coaching. She is a Faculty member of the International Academy for Professional Development, specialising in solution focused cognitive behavioural coaching. She is registered with the Health Professions Council and Chartered with the British Psychological Society (BPS), and is a member of the Association for Coaching (MAC), International Society for Coaching Psychologists (MISCP) and BPS Special Group in Coaching Psychology (SGCP). Initially qualified as an occupational psychologist, Helen gained over ten years' commercial experience working with SHL. Helen and Stephen Palmer developed the CLARITY coaching model and have co-authored articles and chapters on coaching in organisations, solution focused coaching, cognitive behavioural coaching, self-acceptance and stress management.

Foreword

Dr Alasdair J. Macdonald, Consultant Psychiatrist and Family Therapist

After 22 years in solution focused work in the UK and abroad, I was most interested to hear that this book was on its way. I am honoured to be asked to write a Foreword. Around the world in recent years there have been a large number of books published on coaching in general. There have been some texts on solution focused and cognitive-behavioural approaches to coaching. However, this is one of the first UK publications addressing the specific details of how to carry out solution focused coaching. The discovery of the solution focused model was first made in the field of individual and family therapy, so many of the original concepts arise from the therapy setting. However, as this book shows, this new learning has been adapted and extended within the organisational and coaching field.

The three authors are an eminent group. Bill O'Connell is the Director of Training at Focus on Solutions and was the originator of the first master's degree in Solution Focused Therapy (formerly at the University of Birmingham). I have known Bill for many years and never failed to be impressed by his erudition and his humanity. Stephen Palmer is an established academic with a wide range of publications and interests. I admire his ability to see at once to the essence of a problem. The third author, Helen Williams, has an impressive track record. Having provided psychological services within a large organisation for ten years, she is well-qualified to comment on the real-world applications of coaching in such settings. She and Stephen Palmer have been close colleagues on a number of projects.

As one would expect, the book is laid out in a logical progression, starting with coaching as a concept and then moving to the specifics of solution focused coaching practice. Applications in group and team settings are considered, followed by an examination of ways to integrate solution focused practice with other forms of coaching methodology. This includes suggestions to coaches who use other models about how they might usefully introduce some solution focused ideas and techniques into their current work. The final chapter presents 14 exercises to use with individuals and groups within the solution focused model. These are drawn with acknowledgement from a wide variety of practitioners and models and are then adapted to the solution focused context. The text is lucidly and plainly written, with helpful examples of dialogue from real-life coaching sessions.

The chapters include some useful micro-skills of interviewing, with an emphasis on effective ways to use language ('why?', 'could' not 'should'). These show that solution focused coaching may be simple in concept but it is not easy. There is a timely warning to coaches in Chapter 3 about remembering to allow the coachee moments of silence to think through ideas. This differs from the therapy setting in which silence is often over-used, partly as a consequence of the therapy style of more traditional thinkers such as Freud.

Any coach will find something of value in this book, even if they do not decide to adopt the complete solution focused model. They can safely begin to experiment, by using the ideas described so clearly in this book. You cannot guarantee results in human affairs, whether the issues are health, love or money. However, the solution focused approach may now be regarded as of proven value, producing good results in many settings and saving time into the bargain. I hope that many coaches will buy this book and benefit from the wisdom within.

Alasdair J. Macdonald
Weymouth, 2012

Preface

The past decade has been an exciting time for the development of coaching, coaching psychology and mentoring practice around the world. Coaching has gradually shifted from an industry to profession thanks to the work of the professional bodies and their dedicated volunteer members and staff. Some countries or regions such as the United Kingdom have National Occupational Standards, which help to underpin coaching practice in the workplace. Palmer and Whybrow (2007) found that over 28 different approaches to coaching were being used by practitioners. In their on-going surveys up until 2009 they found that solution focused coaching was one of the most popular approaches being used by coaching psychologists.

Why a book on solution focused coaching? We (Bill and Stephen) had already co-edited the *Handbook of Solution Focused Therapy* in 2003, which highlighted how the approach can be used therapeutically in a range of domains or settings such as social work and schools and with different client groups such as parents, children, families and couples. Although we had published papers (Palmer, O'Connell and Grant, 2007) and chapters (O'Connell and Palmer, 2007) on solution focused coaching we realised that although they captured the essence of solution focused coaching practice, we were unable to include the fine detail due to word limitations. There was one obvious solution – a book on solution focused coaching practice. We imagined the desired scenario and got down to work.

Solution Focused Coaching in Practice is a 'how to do it' book. The book does not assume that the reader has any prior knowledge of either coaching or the approach. Therefore we hope that the book will be equally suitable for experienced coaches who may wish to read the chapters specifically on the solution focused approach or neophyte coaches just starting out on their coaching journey. Also we hope that professionals who wish to use a coaching style in their work such as managers, human resource specialists and consultants may find the book useful too.

The first chapter is an introduction to what coaching is in order to set the context. The second chapter provides an overview to solution focused coaching and the following two chapters provide solution focused coaching skills for coaches. Chapter Five then considers the solution focused coach. Chapter Six looks at group and team coaching from a solution focused perspective. Chapter Seven considers practice issues such as the process of solution focused coaching, the coach–coachee relationship, and the role of technology. The next chapter focuses on the inclusive coach who may use techniques, interventions, models and theories drawn from other approaches in a judicious manner. The last chapter provides a range of solution focused coaching exercises, which can be used in individual and group coaching as well as training.

In this book we provide coachee case studies and vignettes that include life, personal and work-related issues. At the end of each chapter we have provided a number of practice tips, discussion issues and suggested reading. In the Appendices we have provided two solution focused coachee worksheets and we have also listed, after the references, useful web resources.

Acknowledgements

First and foremost, I wish to acknowledge the immense help Moira, my wife, gives me in all that I do. I so appreciate and value her input to this book and to our business and family. Thanks also to Donnamarie, Katrina, Joanne and John who support me so well. I have been fortunate in having so many great colleagues who have helped to shape my thinking and writing. I am indebted to the work of Steve de Shazer, Insoo Kim Berg and Bill O'Hanlon and many other Solution Focused writers and practitioners. Discovering the Solution Focused community has been a life-changing event. I would like to mention in particular Steve Conlon, Peter Creagh and Garrath Ford, my colleagues in Focus on Solutions who share their ideas so generously. My college's motto was 'to teach is to learn,' hence my thanks go to the many people who have participated in my training courses over the years and who have contributed greatly to the development of my Solution Focused work.

Bill O'Connell

I thank my colleagues Bill O'Connell, Alasdair Macdonald and Mark McKergow for their reflections on solution focused practice and on-going support over the past decade. Routledge staff have supported my work since 1997, which is much appreciated. Particular thanks go to Joanne Forshaw, the Senior Editor whose on-going patience is remarkable and Kate Moysen, Senior Production Editor who worked with me on this book and others over the years.

Stephen Palmer

I would like to thank Stephen Palmer and Bill O'Connell for the great opportunity to co-author this book with them, which I hope will be of value to others. Thanks also to Stephen for sharing his coaching experience and for involving me in numerous coaching writing projects over the past five years. Special love and thanks to the Marsh, Smith, Frost and Williams families, for all their kindness and support over the years.

Helen Williams

What is coaching?

The modern-day practice of coaching has its origins in early sports coaching, where the aim was to improve the performance of top athletes. From around the 1970s these methods began to be adapted for life and workplace coaching, with the aim of improving perceived quality of life, motivation, task performance and goal achievement; although somewhat surprisingly, workplace performance coaching research can be found in the academic literature as far back as the 1930s (e.g. Gorby, 1937). In the past two decades coaching has become increasingly popular and is now recognised as an effective route to both personal and career development.

Whether the entirety of a person's work as a coach, or as a philosophy or style adopted in order to deliver other objectives, such as managing people and teams, coaching takes many forms. A number of definitions of coaching exist (see Palmer and Whybrow, 2007), a selection of which include:

Unlocking a person's potential to maximise their own performance. It is helping them to learn rather than teaching them (Whitmore, 2002: 8)

The art of facilitating the performance, learning and development of another (Downey, 1999: 15)

Collaborative, individualised, solution focused, results-oriented, systemic and stretching: it fosters self-directed learning (Grant, 2007: 25)

Solution focused, results-oriented systematic process in which the coach facilitates the enhancement of work performance and the self-directed learning and personal growth of the coachee (Grant, 2001: 8)

Solution focused coaching is an outcome-oriented, competence-based approach (O'Connell and Palmer, 2007: 278)

Coaching is in essence about facilitating others to help themselves to attain a desired goal or future state. The majority of coaching methods are non-directive, although some acknowledge a place for more challenging, direct questioning within a non-directive framework.

What coaching is not

The field of coaching shares its boundaries with other practices, and is perhaps most closely linked to the fields of counselling, mentoring and training. For this reason, as well as describing what coaching is, it may also be useful to describe what coaching is not. Coaching is a facilitative approach intended to help the individual achieve work and personal life goals (Grant and Palmer, 2002), focusing on the growth and development of psychologically well individuals (Peltier, 2001). Coaching is not a therapeutic approach for use with individuals wishing to resolve clinical goals or pathological conditions (Grant, 2001; Peltier, 2001), such as depression or paranoia. Where it becomes apparent that the coachee's goals are of a clinical nature, it is appropriate and ethical for the coach to refer the individual, for example to a psychologist or psychotherapist. The key differences between counselling and coaching are summarised in Table 1.1.

Mentoring is typically characterised by a more informal relationship over longer periods of time, with greater

Table 1.1 Counselling and coaching

Counselling	Coaching
Clinical goals	Non-clinical goals
Delivered by a trained counsellor or psychotherapist	Delivered by a trained coach/coaching psychologist
Approach underpinned by a medical model	Approach underpinned by a non-medical, coaching model

emphasis on the transfer of knowledge, imparting of advice and provision of opportunities for personal or career development (Grant, 2001; Jarvis, 2004). By comparison, in coaching the coachee is held responsible for their goals and actions, while 'the coach facilitates learning in the coachee' (Grant, 2001: 7). The ultimate aim is for the coachee to become self-sufficient through internalisation of the coaching tools and techniques. The key differences between mentoring and coaching are summarised in Table 1.2.

Training is commonplace in the workplace for both acquisition of technical skills and development of behavioural competencies. In terms of broader life goals, there are a number of courses available covering numerous aspects of personal development, such as assertiveness skills, time management and presentation skills. Unlike coaching, the intention in training is typically to transfer knowledge and skills from the trainer to the training participant, and as such training tends to be facilitator-centred, with one or two trainers delivering the programme to a group of individuals. The key differences between training and coaching are summarised in Table 1.3.

Table 1.2 **Mentoring and coaching**

Mentoring	Coaching
Informal and directive	Formal and non-directive
Non-specified timeframe	Specified, contracted timeframe
Transfer of knowledge	Progress towards coachee's goals
Creation and/or provision of opportunities for development and career progression	Creation of a safe environment for personal development or job performance

Table 1.3 **Training and coaching**

Training	Coaching
Directive	Non-directive
Facilitator-centred	Coachee-centred
Working to the trainer's agenda	Working to the coachee's agenda
Transfer of knowledge and skills	Progress towards coachee's goals and internalisation of coaching skills

The coaching context

Coaching may take place for a variety of reasons and in a variety of different contexts. An individual may engage a coach to support them in personal development or life coaching goals. An organisation may engage a coach to work with an employee or number of employees on job performance or organisationally driven goals. Coaching might be established at the individual level for personal development, at the group/team level for team development or at the organisational level for the creation of a coaching culture. The coaching context may also be informed by the organisational level of the employee/s, whether intended for call centre staff, the graduate population, middle management, senior management and the leadership team or the executive board. Box 1.1 provides a list of potential objectives for work place coaching.

Box 1.1 Objectives of coaching

- Acquisition of skills.
- Improved performance on a task.
- Transformation of the coachee's life focus.
- Enhanced self-awareness.
- Enhanced self-confidence, self-esteem and/or self-efficacy.
- Competency-based personal development.
- Job transition and career development.
- Improved team performance.
- Cross-cultural awareness.

Who is the coach?

Coaching in organisations is typically delivered by external or internal coaches, managers or members of the HR department (CIPD, 2007). There are a variety of factors for consideration in the selection of a coach (see Jarvis, 2004; Chapman, 2006):

- Internal/external resources available and appropriateness regarding issues of confidentiality.
- Coach qualifications, experience, membership of professional coaching bodies and testimonials.
- Relevance of coaching methods offered for specified coaching goals.
- Fit of interpersonal style to the coachee and organisational culture.

There is a wealth of literature describing the basic skills of coaching (see Whitmore, 1992; Graham, Wedman and Garvin-Kester, 1994; Alexander and Renshaw, 2005; Bresser and Wilson, 2006), which typically include rapport building, questioning, listening and facilitation as well as session and boundary management. A number of professional bodies have been established around the practice of coaching (see Williams and Palmer, 2009), many of which have developed standards frameworks and codes of practice, coach competencies, guidelines for supervision and course recognition and accreditation processes (Jarvis, 2005; Wilson, 2006). Box 1.2 provides a list of example coach competencies.

Box 1.2 Example coach competencies

- Self-awareness, continued professional development and supervision.
- Working to ethical and professional standards.
- Relationship building.
- Effective communication.
- Facilitation of learning and development.
- Goal, outcome and action orientation.
- Application of coaching knowledge, models and techniques.
- Coaching evaluation.

For full details of coach competency frameworks see the Association for Coaching (2005), International Coach Federation (2008) and the European Mentoring and Coaching Council (2009). Do note that these frameworks get updated and it is worth checking their websites for the most recent versions. The United Kingdom also has National Occupational Standards for Coaching and Mentoring.

As an individual coach, it can be an extremely valuable process to reflect on and map out your coaching model and offering: What are your underlying values and philosophies as a coach? What are your qualifications and experiences? What coaching models, tools and techniques do you make use of, and how do you link these together in your own integrative coaching framework? What coaching methods sit outside of your coaching offering? What is your interpersonal and coaching style? Which professional bodies are you a member of and how do you demonstrate that you adhere to their best practice guidelines and standards? Where are your strengths and areas of development as a coach? This clarity will enable you to communicate your coaching model and offering to others, and to deliver coaching with your own unique, authentic style.

We recommend taking a solution focused coaching approach to this exercise. The remainder of this book will detail the solution focused coaching approach in full. In essence, the principles that apply here are:

- Focus on you and your potential as a coach (your coaching skills, experience, values and attitudes).
- Clarify your hopes, goals and aspirations as a coach.
- Consider how you might tap into your resources even more in order to achieve these goals. Remember small steps make a big difference.
- Challenge any negative self-talk.
- Focus on your preferred future as a coach, and consider how you can do more of what works!
- Clarify your immediate action plans and next steps.

Core coaching skills

Two core skills are widely recognised to provide the foundations for effective coaching:

1 Questioning.
2 Listening.

There are a number of different types of questions effectively used in coaching:

- *Open questions* To encourage dialogue, e.g. what, where, when, how, tell me more, describe . . .
- *Closed questions* To reflect back or facilitate a 'yes' response from the coachee, e.g. so what you are describing is; and you would like to think differently on this issue?
- *Socratic questioning* To challenge the evidence for negative or unhelpful thoughts, e.g. what is the evidence for/ against that belief; has there been a time when that wasn't the case; to what extent is holding this belief helpful to you?
- *Scaling questions* Used frequently in solution focused coaching to rate the scale of the problem or level of confidence in dealing with the problem, e.g. on a scale of one to ten where one is not significant, and ten is highly significant, how would you rate this problem?

The art of listening is perhaps harder than it initially seems. Often, when we think we are listening to the person speaking to us, we are in fact only partially attending to them. We are distracted by other sounds and sights, by other thoughts in our heads (oh no, I forgot to pick up the dry cleaning; we really need to be moving this coaching session to a close . . .), by our presumptions about what the person is going to say next or by our own answers to the question posed (surely the next step is obvious . . .).

There are two forms of listening that are instrumental in effective coaching:

1 Active listening.
2 Reflective listening.

Active listening requires the coach to be fully present in the moment, silently and non-judgementally listening to what the person is saying and doing, and to what they are not saying and doing. It is also about observing and acknowledging their own reactions to the situation and the impact this is having on the course of conversation.

Reflective listening is where the coach reflects back, or mirrors, what the coachee has just said. This can be a very powerful way of making the person feel listened to, or of demonstrating that you are listening and encouraging the coachee to reflect on or talk more about the topic raised. You might choose to reflect back the exact words that the coachee has used, to summarise what the coachee has said, or to use a metaphor that helps the coachee to view their situation from a slightly different perspective (Palmer and Burton, 1996).

The coach–client relationship

The coach–client relationship is a fundamental aspect of all coaching engagements (O'Broin and Palmer, 2007; Palmer and McDowall, 2010) and has been found to have significant impact upon likely success of coaching (Stober and Grant, 2006; Stober, Wildflower and Drake, 2006). It is the responsibility of the coach to monitor the dynamics of the coaching relationship, and to raise it as a point of discussion with the coachee if it does not seem to be working. While initially uncomfortable, this discussion may act as a catalyst to removing the barriers within the relationship, or may lead to the coach and coachee agreeing a more suitable solution such as identification of an alternative coach.

The scenario presented above on coaching relationship dynamics is something that might usefully be raised in supervision, to help you as the coach clarify the best way forward. The value of supervision for coaches is increasingly recognised, with the clear benefits of learning, development and a place to discuss ethical issues or concerns (McDougall, 2008).

Who is the client?

Clearly the client is the coachee who has contracted with the coach and who is going to undertake the coaching assignment. However, within organisational settings, this is often less clear-cut. When coaching staff or executives, it is important to clarify who your coaching contract is with. Triad coach contract agreements are common, whereby you (the coach) agree coaching objectives, coaching process, feedback procedures and confidentiality arrangements with both the coachee and their manager and/or HR representative. This will foster a climate in which the coachee is able to trust the confidentiality of the relationship, and/or be aware of its limitations. It also ensures that pressure is not applied at a later date on you (the coach) to share confidential information.

The organisation representative also needs to be aware that the coaching process may lead to outcomes that do or do not align to the organisation's goals, for example if the coaching results in the coachee deciding for themselves that the most appropriate solution for them sits outside of the current organisation.

Key features of coaching

While a number of coaching approaches and models exist, there seems to be a shared understanding of the ultimate goals of:

1 Personal/team/organisational insight.
2 Progressive actionable change.

There also seems to be an underlying formal and structured coaching process that provides the foundations for the industry as a whole. This structure helps coachees to understand what they might expect from coaching, focusing the attention and motivation of both coach and coachee.

A typical coaching process has a beginning, middle and end. The goals and objectives of the coaching are typically agreed at the initial contracting meeting and reviewed at the end of the process. While solution focused coaching does not advocate prescribing the number of coaching sessions, three to five sessions may be found to be required on average. If the manager is acting as coach, then he/she will need to contract with the coachee/s how and when the coaching will take place. For example, will these form separate meetings or will the coaching approach be integrated more informally into regular meetings and performance reviews? Coaching assignments are often agreed between the coach and coachee, for the coachee to complete in-between sessions.

Theoretical approaches to coaching

Although this book is about solution focused coaching, we thought it useful to give some consideration to the wider coaching context. There are indeed a number of different approaches to coaching, and the reason for this can be understood in terms of the different philosophical and theoretical foundations from which they have grown. Perspectives on human learning and development include behaviourist, cognitive (both rationalist and constructivist), psychodynamic, humanist, person-centred, ontological, gestalt, systems theory, transactional analysis, neuro-linguistic programming (NLP), transpersonal, existential, mindfulness, positive psychology and more – and from each perspective comes a considered and useful coaching approach!

While some approaches are quite distinct, others might be viewed as having a great deal in common. Proponents of each approach have, over time, developed their own sets of models, tools and techniques. Approaches that take into consideration both behavioural (practical) and cognitive or emotional (psychological) aspects of a situation have been described as 'multimodal' approaches (Lazarus, 1984; 1989), as well as 'dual systems' approaches i.e. practical and psychological (Neenan and Dryden, 2002; Palmer and Szymanska, 2007).

Solution focused coaching in its purest form has been described as taking a minimalist approach to theory and concepts, directing attention to what is already working in the coachee's life (O'Connell and Palmer, 2007). Increasingly, however, many coaches are considering an inclusive approach, with the integration of theoretical perspectives and blending of coaching approaches (O'Connell, 2005) for practical, efficient, client-centred coaching solutions. In Chapter Eight we consider the inclusive approach to solution focused coaching in more detail.

For more information on the range of theoretical approaches to coaching see Peltier (2001) *The Psychology of Executive Coaching*; Stober and Grant (Eds) (2006) *Evidence Based Coaching Handbook*; Passmore (Ed.) (2006) *Excellence in Coaching*; Palmer and Whybrow (Eds) (2007) *Handbook of*

Coaching Psychology; and Cox, Bachkirova and Clutterbuck (Eds) (2010) *The Complete Handbook of Coaching*.

The value of coaching

There is a growing body of academic research with findings in support of the value and effectiveness of coaching (see Kampa-Kokesch and Anderson, 2001; Grant, 2006b; Passmore and Gibbes, 2007). The Association for Coaching published a survey reporting benefits to the individual including improved managerial skills, enhanced motivation and improved work–life balance (AC, 2004). Benefits at the team and organisational level have been found to include increased team working and leadership skills, improved performance and reduction of workplace stress (Gonzalez, 2004; Gyllensten and Palmer, 2005; Cortvriend, Harris and Alexander, 2008).

Managing change through coaching

Whether at the individual, team or organisational level, coaching is a fundamental tool in the facilitation of change. The coaching process affords the individual or group of individuals an opportunity to heighten awareness of self, others and the environment. Awareness facilitates choice, and the act of choosing enhances perceived control and subsequent levels of engagement and commitment to the process of change.

Practice tips

- Reflect on your coaching practice:
    - In which coaching contexts do you provide coaching?
    - What, if any, theoretical framework do you model your coaching on?
    - How do you describe coaching to others?
    - What coaching do you provide?
    - What coaching do you not provide?

- Consider a solution focused approach to your own continued professional development (CPD) as a coach:

- What are your coach competencies?
- Where are your strengths?
- How might you develop your coaching practice by doing something different?

• Establish clear contracts around confidentiality and feedback processes.

Discussion points

• Do you believe there are really differences between coaching and mentoring?
• In your opinion, what are the key features of coaching?
• What are your concerns, if any, about coaching staff within organisations?
• Can a manager be a coach?

Suggested reading

Cox, E., Bachkirova, T. and Clutterbuck, D. (Eds) (2010) *The Complete Handbook of Coaching*. London: Sage Publications.

Palmer, S. and McDowall, A. (2010) *The Coaching Relationship: Putting People First*. Hove: Routledge.

Palmer, S. and Panchal, S. (2011) *Developmental Coaching: Life Transitions and Generational Perspectives*. Hove: Routledge.

Palmer, S. and Whybrow, A. (Eds) (2007) *Handbook of Coaching Psychology: A Guide for Practitioners*. London: Routledge.

Palmer, S., Grant, A. and O'Connell, B. (2007) Solution focused coaching: Lost and found. *Coaching at Work*, 2(4): 22–29.

Peltier, B. (2010) *The Psychology of Executive Coaching: Theory and Application* (2nd edition). New York: Routledge.

Stober, D.R. and Grant, A.M. (Eds) (2006) *Evidence Based Coaching Handbook: Putting Best Practices to Work for your Clients*. Hoboken, NJ: Wiley.

2

An overview of solution focused coaching

Introduction

Which features of the solution focused approach make it suitable for coaching?

- It is positive and practical.
- It is time-efficient and cost effective.
- It focuses clearly on specific, measurable outcomes.
- It energises the coachee to own the process and the outcomes.
- It is simple without being simplistic.
- It is capacity-building.
- It is transparent and the skills are transferable.

Its popularity as a therapeutic tool used by thousands of professionals and its extensive use with a wide range of clients, in many different contexts and cultures, is of course in itself a recommendation.

Does the solution focused approach work? Dr Alasdair MacDonald, Research Officer of the European Brief Therapy Association, cites 71 relevant studies covering a wide range of client groups. Most, but not all of these studies concern its use in a therapeutic context. A review of all available research can be found at www.solutionsdoc.co.uk. In his analysis of these studies, McDonald (2007) concludes that, 'Solution Focused Therapy can claim to be the equal of other psychotherapies, while also taking less time and resources for treatment' (2007: 113). Green and her associates' (2006) study examined a ten-week Life Coaching Programme using a combination of the solution focused and the cognitive-behavioural approach. Although there were clear limits to the study, the results suggested that the programme had significantly increased participants' goal striving, subjective well-being, psychological well-being and hope.

The solution focused approach is light on explicit theory. It aims to be minimalist in its concepts and interventions, following William of Occam, a fourteenth-century scholar, who formulated the axiom that an explanation for a phenomenon should make as few assumptions as possible. In other words we should look for the simplest explanation first. This minimalism leads the coach to 'join with' what is already working in the person's life, rather than feel it is necessary to start with a blank sheet. Solution focused coaching is an ethical process guided by specific beliefs and values.

Basic belief

A fundamental belief in solution focused coaching is that people are more likely to change and achieve their goals quickly when they tap into their own resources and solutions. It assumes that coachees are already using their resources to implement solutions in their lives, although they may not be aware of this. The task for the coach is to encourage them to discover what works for them, reinforce their solutions and question how they could expand their solution repertoire. It also assumes that although coachees are skilled problem-solvers, they are unlikely to be using more than a fraction of their potential. They will, for example, have forgotten many of the solutions that worked for them in the past. They will have transferable skills that are not being used because they have not yet recognised their potential usefulness. These assumptions have the potential to become self-fulfilling prophecies.

In the light of these assumptions the coach adopts the following principles:

- *Work with the person not the problem.*
  The coach engages with a unique human being who has a specific set of values, attitudes, skills and experiences. A

solution focused coach, along with coaches using other approaches, will attempt to find ways of co-operating with each coachee, taking into account their learning style. The prevailing themes of the meetings will be the capacity and the potential of the coachee. Their problems, weaknesses and deficits will be of secondary interest. (In fact it is usually better to view 'weaknesses' as 'skills deficits,' which can be improved if necessary.)

- *People have many ideas about their preferred futures.*
  Despite the sheer unpredictability of life and the lack of control we have over our future, it is part of human nature to attempt to anticipate, predict and work towards a desired future. Coachees may have vague aspirations as to what precisely they want. They may be unclear as to how much they want it or how much they are willing to invest in order to achieve it.

- *Focus on the future not the past.*
  We are clearly the product of our history and need to learn the lessons that it teaches us. Although the emphasis in solution focused coaching is on 'what's going to happen next,' we can retrieve transferable skills and solutions from what's already happened. Reflection upon our personal histories can also reveal inherited scripts, which are either part of the solution, or part of the problem.

- *Avoid paralysis by analysis.*
  It is possible to think too much! For some people this is an escape from doing something. A pre-occupation with finding explanations and theories about a current situation as an essential condition before taking action is often a recipe for inertia. It may also set off a search for someone or something to blame. Disagreement over the causes of a problem can lead to self-justifying behaviour and further deterioration in the situation.

- *Ask questions, rather than offer answers.*
  The solution focused coach leads from behind, encouraging the coachee to prioritise practical solutions that can be immediately put into practice.

- *Examine negative self-talk.*
  Negative self-talk can de-motivate and block a coachee from achieving their goals. The solution focused coach listens out for negative self-talk and brings it to the coachee's attention if necessary. The coachee is encouraged to develop realistic thinking (not positive thinking) instead to counter the negative self-talk.

- *Listen for and reinforce the person's strengths and resources.*
  The solution focused coach highlights and reinforces the coachee's strengths and resources. The coachee may be encouraged to note them down in order to remind him/herself that they already possess some key attributes. This process helps the development of self-efficacy.

- *If it's working, keep doing it.*
  Generally speaking, it is more useful to build on 'what works' than to ask someone to do something entirely new and different (although there is also a time for doing something different). The fact that the person has already successfully handled a situation provides an opportunity for them to reflect upon how they did it and to be encouraged to do it again. Where they have already accomplished something that is more difficult than the action they are about to undertake, the evidence is even more compelling.

- *If it's not working, stop it and do something different.*
  We are often attached to our solutions, even when they are proven to be failures. We keep doing them in the hope that one day they may come good and produce the result we want – a triumph of hope over experience (Oscar Wilde). We will do this ignoring the fact that on the whole, 'if you always do what you've always done, you'll always get what you've got.' Abandoning our failed solutions opens up the possibility that we might find an alternative that might be worth trying instead.

- *Explore 'solutions' to maximise learning.*
  It's useful to find solutions, but of limited value if they are soon forgotten. Coaching is a means to capture 'the

difference that makes the difference' in a way that will allow the coachee to replicate it.

- *If it isn't broken, don't fix it, unless it can be improved.*
  Overeager coaches may actually be unethically invading their coachees' privacy by encouraging them to disclose irrelevant problems. There needs to be a clear boundary between coaching and therapy and for practitioners to keep within their remit.

  Although this principle of leaving what is not broken alone is helpful, there are limits to it as well. The time to improve performance may be when things are going well and we can see what is needed to bring continuing success. Resting on one's laurels may result in being overtaken and left behind. Some people stay in their comfort zone when they are capable of much more. Success often lies in paying attention to details and making micro-improvements in every area of performance. Leaving well alone does not exclude the need for maintenance of what is working; otherwise sooner or later it will cease to be effective.

- *Small steps, big difference.*
  One small step at a time is often the way to go. For many people, the first step is the hardest. The solution focused coaching approach is to agree upon a small, but significant, starting point. This step may even constitute a breakthrough event for the individual. An initial success may create momentum, so that small steps add up to one long jump!

  Some coachees are willing to take big steps, and that's fine, as long as they are ready and not setting themselves up for failure. Others gain confidence by seeing the benefits as they move forward slowly and surely. Generating hope is an important ingredient in effective coaching. A skilled coach will also be aware of highly competitive coachees who are driven in the pursuit of their goals. They are re-enacting in the coaching relationship the very attitudes and behaviours which got them into difficulties in the first place. Taking small steps forward should not preclude attention to the bigger picture.

Sometimes, absorption in minutiae is the enemy of progress.

The origins of the solution focused approach

The origins of the solution focused approach lie in family therapy. It emerged in the 1980s from the work of a group of practitioners at the Brief Therapy Centre in Milwaukee, led by Steve De Shazer and Insoo Kim Berg. Since then, practitioners in fields such as mentoring and teaching, counselling, coaching, mediation, mental health, primary care, substance misuse, social work, psychology and business have adopted it and adapted it to different contexts and groups (see O'Connell and Palmer, 2003).

The families coming to the Brief Therapy Centre often presented with multiple and complex problems. Family members would argue among themselves about what exactly the problem was and who was to blame for it. This could take up a lot of time. In this arena of conflict and hostility family members were understandably defensive, and as a result, were typically unable or unwilling to make personal changes. Observing this unproductive stand-off led to the team changing tack. Instead of trying to create a consensus around the family's problems, the team tried instead to find agreement around what the solutions would look like. They asked each family member how they would know the situation had improved – what would they notice that was different? With this starting point, the team found that families spent less time arguing over their problems. They discovered that when they encouraged family members to notice times when things were better, the family made more progress and faster. As the family focused more on 'solutions,' they became less trapped in the vicious circle generated by focusing on the problem. The therapists gave clients evidence-based 'compliments' which reinforced their solutions-behaviour and asked them challenging questions to help them expand their repertoire.

Clients seemed to engage better with this approach and to make more changes more quickly. Yet the solutions they began to implement often seemed unrelated to the presenting problems. Somehow it didn't seem to matter. What was important was that clients began to 'do something different.' They broke the hold that the problem pattern had over them and discovered that they had the resources to shape a better future.

De Shazer was greatly influenced by the ground-breaking seminal work of the therapist Milton Erickson. Erickson was extremely successful in helping people to change. He would utilise everything that the client could bring – their skills, their mistakes, their beliefs, their idio-syncrasies. He would change his approach to fit each client. He regarded everyone he saw as a skilled problem-solver who had the resources to find solutions that would work for them. Since in his view, change is constant, there must be times when people 'do their problem differently.' These occasions are described in solution focused coaching as 'exceptions.' Erickson used hypnotherapy to facilitate clients to imagine their preferred future, then encourage them to be amnesiac about the experience (O'Hanlon and Weiner-Davis, 2003). He found that many clients managed to rid themselves of their problems through this and other techniques he used. Erickson used pre-suppositional questions, which are a form of unconscious suggestion that assume that the future desired event has or will happen. Such questions figure prominently in solution focused coaching. These interventions will be examined in more detail in chapters Three and Four.

The SOLUTION coaching model

The SOLUTION coaching model (Williams *et al.*, 2011), depicted in Figure 2.1, provides the basic structure of a solution focused coaching meeting. The amount of time spent on each intervention will vary. A first session is likely to require more time to clarify the coachee's hopes and goals. Some coachees may find the visualisation of their preferred future through the use of the Miracle Question (de Shazer, 1988) so helpful that they use a whole session to explore their answers to it. Later sessions may focus exclusively on evaluating and expanding solutions.

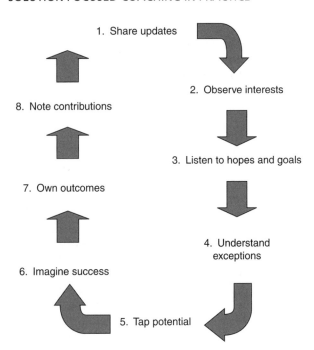

Figure 2.1 **The SOLUTION coaching model**

The SOLUTION coaching model encompasses eight stages of solution focused coaching as follows.

1 *Share updates*
   For the solution focused coach the work begins prior to the first meeting, as coachees are asked to notice any positive changes they have made in the interval between making the appointment and coming to the meeting. In the first step of the model coachees are invited to reflect on and talk through any pre-meeting change they have noticed.

2 *Observe interests*
   This stage of solution focused coaching is most commonly referred to as 'problem-free talk,' and provides an opportunity for the coach to get to know the coachee as a person

with varied interests and preferences. By listening to the coachee as they discuss hobbies and interests, both coach and coachee may observe key strengths and sources of motivation that might be of great benefit to the coachee if applied to their current challenge or problem.

3 *Listen to hopes and goals*

The coachee is highly likely to need to spend time initially talking through the current challenge or problem as they perceive it. It is important to engage in 'problem-talk' for as long as the coachee needs. Taking a solution focused approach does not mean that problems and concerns are ignored, denied or overlooked. On the contrary, an important part of solution focused coaching is the validation of the individual and any concerns that they might have. The solution focused coach listens to the coachee, gradually encouraging them to shift their focus from the present problem onto their hopes and goals, laying the foundations for consideration of potential solutions. When ready, coachees are encouraged to explore their aspirations and future-focused goals and to begin to think about what resources they already have to assist them.

4 *Understand exceptions*

A key principle in solution focused coaching is the belief that the individual has access to the best solutions to their problems, although they might not be conscious of this at the start of the coaching engagement. The best solution might be something that they used to resolve a past challenge successfully, a 'signature strength' that they utilise often but have not yet thought to apply to the current problem, or a willingness to have a go at something different and new. In order to discover old solutions and/ or signature solutions, ask questions to understand exceptions to the current challenge or problem: when has the situation been better or different; have there been times when the problem was not present; when has the coachee been in a similar situation and reacted differently, leading to more positive outcomes; what was different about these situations; how were they thinking, feeling and acting; what strengths, skills and resources did they use?

5 *Tap potential*

Throughout the conversation the coach reflects back evidence of the coachee's transferable skills, strengths, solutions and signature solutions, competencies and other resources (Williams *et al.*, 2011). The coach encourages the coachee to consider how they might tap into this potential to solve their current problem or challenge.

6 *Imagine success*

The purpose of this stage is for the coachee to imagine what their preferred future looks like (Williams *et al.*, 2011). Imagery can be a powerful tool for enhancing the clarity of a goal, and for re-establishing a person's motivation and drive to achieve that goal. De Shazer's (1988) Miracle Question is key here, and is discussed in more detail in Chapter Three. This may be worded flexibly to suit the needs of the coachee, for example: waking to find their problem solved, what do they notice that is different; how are they thinking, feeling and behaving; what is the response from others? (Williams *et al.*, 2011).

7 *Own outcomes*

By the end of the meeting the next steps forward are usually evident. This stage in the discussion is to help the coachee clarify the next steps to be taken in order to make progressive step-change towards their chosen solution(s). What small steps might they take; what is the first step to be taken; on a scale of one to ten, where ten is completely confident, how confident does the coachee feel; if confidence is less than a seven, what needs to change to make them feel more confident? Encourage the coachee to own these outcomes by choosing the next steps for themselves. A 'notice assignment' might be useful whereby the coachee non-judgementally observes the progress they make with these steps and the impact it has for themselves and others.

8 *Note contributions*

Appreciative feedback is an important tool in the solution focused coaching toolkit. This final stage in the discussion provides the coach with an opportunity to reflect back the progress the coachee has made prior to

and during the meeting, and to note the positive contributions made to the session. It is also an opportunity to seek
appreciative feedback on the coaching session itself, to
see what has worked well and what might be done differently in the future (Williams *et al.*, 2011). In solution
focused coaching, it is commonplace to view each
coaching session as complete within itself; to check
whether the coaching goals have been met, and whether
or not any further coaching meetings are required.

The coach is responsible for maintaining the structure of the
session. Consistently following the same conversational
map helps the coach to keep the focus. It is a navigational
tool to ensure that the participants keep on track and that
the conversation does not drift off into unhelpful areas.
Confidence comes from doing something well on a regular
basis. The more often the coach sees the value of using the
map, the more skilled he or she becomes. After a time, the
map becomes internalised into the coach's relationship style
and can be revisited periodically in supervision.

The solution focused approach is usually described as
'brief.' Clients receiving solution focused therapy typically
make lasting changes in three to five sessions, considerably
fewer sessions than in most other therapies.

The main features of brief, focused coaching are:

- A focus on the here and now.
- Clear, specific and attainable goals.
- Projection of confidence and competence by coach.
- A good working relationship established as soon as
possible.
- A coach who is active and influential.
- A commitment from coachees to work on their goals
between the meetings.

Underpinning the approach is the following set of values.

Trust

Solution focused coaches trust coachees to use their expertise to achieve their goals. Their 'inside' knowledge is

crucial to achieving outcomes. We liken the relationship between their respective areas of expertise to a global navigation system, which is useful in getting a person from home to an unfamiliar location. It also gives us a route into our city centre that we may not use at peak times. Perhaps there are at least three other better routes to follow. Coachees often know the short cuts to their goals. We can help them to think through their goals and explore various routes to achieve them, but they need to do the 'insider' thinking which makes the difference. Professionals may have the knowledge, but coachees often have the know-how.

As well as trusting the coachee, the coach trusts the process. Experience teaches that if the coach is patient and maintains the focus on solutions, a breakthrough, pivotal moment will come.

Sustainability

Solutions that depend upon the expertise of the coach are of less value than those that enable the coachee to be self-reliant.

Customisation

Formulaic solutions, or 'one size fits all' solutions, are alien to solution focused coaching. People have different learning styles and different signature solutions. It is more productive to join with these than to propose off-the-shelf solutions.

Ownership

The neutral, non-judgemental stance of the solution focused coaching supports coachees' ownership and commitment to their solutions.

The FOCUS coaching model

In Chapter Six we present a five-step solution focused coaching model, 'FOCUS,' which represents a shortened version of the SOLUTION coaching model described above (see Williams *et al.*, 2011). This may be useful for group coaching, and for coachees who are highly familiar with coaching and the solution focused coaching approach. See Chapter Six for more details.

What solution focused coaching is not

Positive thinking

When we ask participants at the start of one of our solution focused training courses what they know about the approach, they often say it is about 'positive thinking.' We can understand how people may have gained that impression, but a competence-based approach is about much more than positive thinking. A healthy awareness of threats and dangers is a survival instinct that has allowed us to evolve as a species. Psychotic optimism is a recipe for extinction.

Problem-solving

Many coaches are skilled problem-solvers. This may be what drew them to coaching in the first place. They care about their coachees. It is tempting to rescue coachees when they see them stuck. There are, however, countless so-called experts eager to sell us solutions to our problems. Advice is cheap and easily dispensed, but often unhelpful.

Most coaches will say that they would never dream of taking over in this way. They aim to work in partnership with their coachees and work out solutions collaboratively. In practice, however, under pressure of time, and perhaps through a personal need to look credible, the temptation is to take short cuts. Instead of being patient and asking questions to draw out the coachee's own unique strategies, the problem-solving coach proposes what the coachee should do. This denies coachees the opportunity to think for themselves, to work out what they need and to develop their own decision-making, problem-solving skills. Solution focused is not a 'quick fix' to patch up a particular problem; it is a view of life and a set of skills to enable people to 'do it themselves.' Literally, to stand on their own two feet.

There are, of course, exceptions to any rule and there are occasions when it is not only right, but essential for a coach to make options clear to the coachee and positively advocate one rather than the other. These occasions could be when the coachee is planning to do something illegal, or is proposing to harm themself or someone else. There are also times when the coachee is unable to mobilise their own resources, and has really 'tried everything they can possibly think of.' In such circumstances it would be unrealistic to maintain the 'back seat' role. As a temporary measure, it may be necessary for the coach to initiate a course of action (even break confidentiality in extreme circumstances) or to make a referral to the appropriate professional.

Solution focused coaching does not attempt to untangle problems. Some coaching approaches consider it essential that problems be examined and understood, before any solutions can be found. But solution focused coaching maintains that this *can* be helpful, although it is not necessary and there is always the danger that if you dwell on the problem you will become an expert – on the problem.

Problems v solutions

Sometimes I lie awake at night and I ask where have I gone wrong?

Then a voice says to me, 'This is going to take more than one night.'

Charlie Brown

Most helping approaches adopt a rationale for explaining the difficulties a person is experiencing. These range from skills deficits, thinking errors to unconscious mechanisms. Explanations, however, are culturally conditioned and go in and out of favour. Explaining the causes can be a starting point for working on a problem, but it is not synonymous with dealing with it. In some cases explanations may provide the excuse for doing nothing. If you think the cause of your failure is something in your past and hence beyond your control, then you may well conclude that there is no point in trying any further. This is particularly the case when the explanation goes to the perceived core of the individual's personality. Failure becomes not an experience from which to learn, but one that confirms the person's already low self-esteem.

We consistently use similar explanations for life events and these are rooted in our fundamental values. However, a major life-changing event can challenge those values and lead to the person seeing the world in a quite different way. The way we 'filter our experiences' and anticipate the future will have been largely formed in our childhood and modified by life experience. Some of these filters will still be useful to us, but others are past their sell-by date and need discarding. One aspect of coaching is to help coachees become aware of these filters and their effect upon how they interpret events, and assist them in modifying those that are causing them difficulties.

Two studies demonstrate the power of problem-focused talk. A study by Rosenkranz and associates (2005) reported that using asthma-related words in interviews with asthma patients produced effects on their brain and lung function. A study by Hausdorff *et al.* (1999) reported that talking about age-related decline to the elderly led to worse gait and intellectual skills.

Being solution focused does not mean that we minimise problems, but there are ways of talking about problems that can exacerbate them and ways of talking about them that can lead to solutions.

Problem talk that may help:

- Getting it off your chest.
- Being believed and understood.
- Not identifying yourself with the problem.
- Seeing the problem as temporary.
- Holding flexible predictions about future developments.
- Having positive assumptions.
- A willingness to see problems as normal.

Problem talk that does not help:

- Blaming and accusing.
- Fatalist and defeatist.

- A rigid view that the problem is permanent and unchanging.
- A belief that 'I am the problem.'
- Taking too much or too little responsibility.
- Unrealistic, irrational thinking.
- Negative assumptions.
- Pessimistic predictions.
- Strong attachment to 'problem identity.'

A coach may be the only person in whom a coachee can confide. Being listened to without being judged, humoured or patronised is for many people an uncommon experience. Talking over issues with a skilled and attentive listener can shed light into corners of our thinking and behaving in a way we probably could not accomplish on our own. The very act of expressing our thoughts and feelings to another human being can act as a 'reality test' and enable us to see the way forward. From a solution focused perspective, I believe that I can be helpful without knowing much at all about the problem, but this does not alter the fact that the coachee may feel the need to tell me. Listening carefully to 'problem talk' is part of relationship building. Paying attention to our problems is an evolutionary instinct. Problems are helpful alerts to situations or behaviours that we need to address in order to stay healthy and safe.

Validating the person

We do this in a number of ways. One is to support their right to their perception of the situation even when you do not agree with them. The coach may use statements such as:

- I can see why that makes sense to you.
- I can appreciate that you would feel like that.
- I can only imagine how difficult it must have been for you.

Example

Coachee: I feel really hard done by; I didn't deserve such a negative appraisal.

Coach: You feel it was unfair.
Coachee: He made me feel that I was doing nothing right. I wondered whether he was setting me up for the push in the next round of redundancies.
Coach: You felt it wasn't justified and that he had another agenda about your future.
Coachee: I may be wrong but that's what I'm wondering.
Coach: I can see that if you thought that was what was happening that you would feel aggrieved about it.

Unless coachees feel validated they are likely to defend themselves and as a consequence be closed to new ideas and initiatives. Another way of showing respect for the experiences, feelings and concerns of coachees is to build on their skills and qualities and not be preoccupied with their weaknesses and deficits.

Solution focused coaches aim to match the language of the coachee and to model solution language. Matching builds rapport while modelling demonstrates a different way of talking and thinking about their situation.

Matching language

Hutchins (1989) suggests that practitioners need to be aware of both their clients' and their own dominant ways of experiencing the world. He identifies these modes as thinking, feeling and acting (TFA). Practitioners become aware of their clients' orientation by paying careful attention to how they talk about their problems. Although we are a mixture of all three elements, we are likely to have a bias towards one or another at a particular time. So if a coachee uses predominantly feeling-oriented language, the coach would respond, at least initially, in kind, in order to get on their wavelength. If the coach was aware that she herself had a dominant 'action-oriented' way of seeing the world she would need to be careful that she did not rush her coachees into premature action plans. If the coach was predominantly a 'thinker' and the client a 'doer,' she would need to ensure that her preference for reflection did not hold the coachee back unduly from action.

Modelling language

In Chapter Four we will look at some of the different ways in which we can influence our coachees to talk constructively about their issues. Using pre-suppositional questions is one example, as this directs coachees towards talking about their desired goals as if they had already happened. Coaches avoid abstract vague terms such as under-achievement or low self-esteem in favour of specific, pictorial, concrete descriptions of behaviour. They encourage coachees to do likewise.

Example

Coachee: It's stressing me out.
Coach: What exactly is happening?
Coachee: I can't sleep, I lie awake at night worrying.
Coach: What else is telling you that you are stressed?
Coachee: I'm not eating properly, just junk food, which makes me feel guilty.
Coach: So two of the signs for you when you are stressed are that you can't sleep for worrying and that you have a bad diet. Anything else?
Coachee: I'm making a lot of mistakes because I've got too much to do.
Coach: Has there been a recent example of that?
Coachee: Yesterday I completely forgot a meeting I was supposed to attend.
Coach: From the three things you've mentioned which will change first when you're not so stressed?
Coachee: It was a bad mistake missing that meeting, it was something of a wake-up call. I can't risk doing that again.
Coach: So what would you need to do to ensure that you didn't get so stressed that you missed any more meetings?
Coach: I need to stop putting things in two diaries. My desk diary had the meeting in it, but my Blackberry didn't.

Neuroscience and solution focused coaching

With so much information bombarding our senses and brains, we need to edit and select what we judge to be most appropriate at the time. We can process information by either focusing on the material that leads to solutions, or by focusing on the material relating to barriers and problems. In either case we tend to find what we are looking for!

We store our experiences of major life events in our long-term memory and are particularly able to access those that have a strong emotional resonance. Johnson (2004) describes the brain as, 'an associative network in which thoughts are represented by groups of neurons distributed throughout our brains that fire in sync with each other. Certain thoughts have more neurons in common than others. Neurons that fire together, wire together' (p.200). When we revisit our memories we trigger off other associated memories. From a solution focused standpoint the consequences of this are that the coach discourages the coachee from revisiting those 'problem' neural connections which the coachee has maintained by dwelling upon their problems. By neglecting the problem pathways the neural connections will become weakened.

Conversely the coach encourages the coachee to build new pathways to solutions. This fires off other neurons associated with memories of solutions in their memory bank. These connections will become stronger the more the coachee thinks and talks about how to make the changes they desire.

When people spend excessive time analysing their problems they strengthen the neural networks attached to the problem memory. Recalling all the details around the problem experience invites the brain to search for associated memories of other problems. This generates the original feelings such as sadness, anxiety, fear or anger. This re-enactment imprints a fresh memory of the problem experience. When these pathways have developed over a long period of time and been regularly re-visited, it becomes difficult to break the connections. Similarly, when a person reflects upon previous successes, transferable skills and resources, the brain automatically seeks evidence of a similar kind. When positive feelings such as joy, satisfaction and pride accompany the memory, the brain logs this rewarding and empowering experience and reinforces the pathways to solutions. This pleasurable effect brings chemical rewards, which in turn motivate the coachee to repeat the 'solution experience.'

Solution focused coaching argues that by dwelling upon disturbance, deficits and problems the individual is likely to attract more of the same. People can be drawn into a 'victim culture,' which can disempower them and leave them passive in the hands of professionals. In contrast to this, solution focused coaching fosters coachee-independence, responsibility and choice. It facilitates self-directed learning by transforming implicit knowledge into explicit know-how. It motivates coachees to overcome the challenges and difficulties they encounter.

Law of requisite variety

In order to mobilise the coachee's resources in actively seeing solutions, the work of the coach may need to comply with the law of requisite variety (Ashby, 1956). The law proposes that the party who has most flexibility or options, will have the most power in the relationship. In a scenario in which a coachee blocks necessary changes, the coach would need to have more 'moves' than the coachee, otherwise a stalemate will result. So the coach must have at least one additional argument than the coachee to rebut his or her objections to the changes. The coach will need to be flexible in adapting to any new challenge the coachee presents.

As an example, let us consider one of the most common responses that a coachee makes to a question from the coach – 'I don't know.'

Coach: So what will be the first sign for you that you are going in the right direction?

Coachee: I don't know. I can't see the woods for the trees at the moment.

Coach: What do you think yourself just off the top of your head?

Coachee: It's hard, I feel as if I've tried just about every-thing and maybe I should just give up on it for now.

Coach: So it feels hard, what would be the smallest step you could take in the next couple of days that might make you more hopeful you could sort it out?

Coachee: I don't know, have you got any ideas?

Coach: Well I probably have, but they may not fit you. You know best what works for you. If you were say one on the scale at the moment and tomorrow you realised you were two what would you notice that was different?

Coachee: I would have stopped being so short-tempered.

Coach: How would you have done that?

Coachee: I'd have gone out for a walk at lunchtime and got away from everyone.

The coach needs to have a wide repertoire of interventions in order to keep stimulating the coachee to think of what she or he could do to start reducing stress levels. When a coach starts to become frustrated with the apparent lack of co-operation, he may start to 'sell solutions' himself. This is nearly always a risky course of action as the coachee may reject them all in turn, taking them both down a cul-de-sac.

Observe and describe

Solution focused coaches aim to help coachees see 'beyond' problems and to focus more clearly on their resources and solutions. Instead of analysing and defining problems, coaches help coachees to change how they perceive and interpret their own and others' behaviour. What they are asked to look out for are what works/what happens to make things better. This attention-shift enables coachees to learn how to maintain or expand the desired changes. When they are encouraged to look out for and pay attention to evidence of constructive change, they are more likely to see it.

The solution focused conversational process is one of moving from problem-talk to solution-talk. In

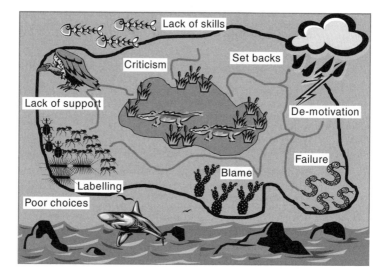

Figure 2.2 **Problem Island**

the illustrations we have described these two types of inter-actions as two separate islands (see O'Connell, 2001). The coachee is 'on Problem Island' (Figure 2.2) where the inter-action is characterised by blame/punishment/failure/de-motivation. Coachees may have spent a lot of time there and have many experiences to relate. In order to escape from Problem Island the coach makes solution-oriented interven-tions, such as asking pre-suppositional questions. These change the focus of attention towards strengths, skills and the possibility of success. Most of the meeting will hopefully take place on Solution Island (Figure 2.3).

Solution focused coaching and change

Solution focused coaching does not propose a particular sequence or pattern of change applicable to all. Instead it proposes that people change more quickly when they focus on what they want to happen next, rather than what has happened already. They make further changes as they become aware of changes already happening in their lives.

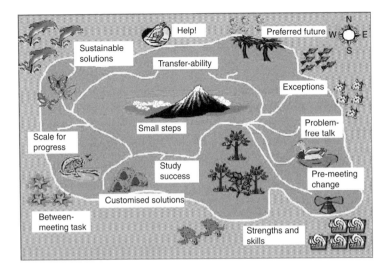

Figure 2.3 Solution Island

When they realise that problems are not fixed, rigid or static, but in a constant state of evolution, they become more hopeful that they can influence events.

People change when they:

- Know *what* to change, *when* to change and *how* to change.
- Believe that there is something better than their present circumstances and that they have the ability to make and sustain change.
- Tap into what is best about themselves.
- Find evidence about which to be hopeful and optimistic.

Change becomes more attractive and attainable when people face it from a position of self-worth (very different from narcissism), believing that they have the capacity to rise to the challenge. Solution focused coaching supports this foundation by giving coachees evidence-based, honest, practical feedback. People are more likely to achieve their goals when they know they have resources at their disposal.

In this chapter we have begun to describe and explain the solution focused coaching approach. These principles, values and interventions ensure that the coach is not merely a technician, but a professional working from an ethical and sustainable philosophy that puts the needs of the coachee centre-stage.

Practice tips

- Always look for what is already working for coachees before you ask them to do something they have never done.
- Work with where coachees are at present, not where you or they would like them to be.
- Small steps, big difference.
- Small steps are the way forward most of the time.
- Be patient and trust the process, opportunities will come.
- Mirror and model language.
- Be conscious of time spent on Problem or Solution Island.
- Being solution focused does not mean that you don't care about peoples' problems.

Discussion points

- Do coachees focus on problem talk more than solution talk initially in coaching?
- How important is it for the coachee to understand eight stages of The SOLUTION coaching model?
- Both the coach and coachee have responsibilities in the coaching session.
- Solution focused coaching has been accused of being light on theory. Can theory help or hinder coaching?

Suggested reading

O'Connell, B. (2001, 2004) *Solution Focused Stress Counselling.* London: Sage Publications.

O'Connell, B. and Palmer, S. (2007) Solution focused Coaching. In S. Palmer and A. Whybrow (Eds) *Handbook of Coaching Psychology: A For Practitioners*, pp.278–292. Hove: Routledge.

Williams, H., Palmer, S. and O'Connell, B. (2011) Introducing SOLUTION and FOCUS: Two solution focused coaching models. *Coaching Psychology International*, 4(1): 6–9.

3

Solution focused skills
for coaches

Introduction

Until the relatively recent arrival of Positive Psychology,
most professional training in the helping professions was
heavily biased towards finding the causes of peoples' problems and ill health and developing interventions to remedy
them; a focus on weaknesses and not on strengths. We knew
a lot about why and how people were sick or unhappy. The
solution focused model fits with the paradigm shift towards
understanding how and why people become and remain
happy and healthy. We have begun to talk the language of
well-being, of strengths and solutions (Berg and Szabó, 2005;
Greene and Grant, 2003).

Changing the habits of a professional lifetime is not
easy. We train many professionals each year in the solution
focused approach and we can see how challenging it can be
for many of them to contain their natural inclination to ask
lots of detailed questions about their clients' problems. It is
only when they experience how helpful it is to invest 80 per
cent of their interviewing time in constructing solutions
with clients and only 20 per cent (at most) on trying to understand the problems that they begin to believe there is a more
useful way of helping their clients.

The content and direction of a coaching meeting is
co-constructed by the coach and the coachee. Underpinning
the solution focused approach is the philosophy of Social
Constructionism, which proposes that meaning is created in
the process of social interaction and negotiation between

people. In Watzlawick's phrase (1984), 'reality is invented, not discovered.' When a coach and a coachee initiate a conversation there is no fixed meaning or objective truth to what is being discussed. Everything is negotiable. Through careful use of language the coach and coachee can reframe their shared communication in a way that enables change to take place more easily. They can either talk up or talk down problems, they can redefine problems, they can talk themselves into a corner or they can talk themselves out of one. Becoming language-sensitive is one of the first things that happens to newcomers to the solution focused approach. They become more aware of the many different ways there are of understanding a person's situation and how some of those lead more easily to solutions than others.

Example

Suzanne:	I don't think I can do this. There is a lot of pressure to get this right and they haven't given me enough time to do it properly.
Coach:	You feel confident about the task but under unrealistic time-pressure.
Suzanne:	I need more time to do it properly. I hate having to hand in work that does not reflect well on me.
Coach:	So you could get it in on time but you feel it wouldn't be up to your standards.
Suzanne:	It would be scrappy. I'd have to leave a lot of stuff out and take shortcuts.
Coach:	Have you ever been in this position before Suzanne?
Suzanne:	Only a few times and I hated it then.
Coach:	What happened when you handed the work in?
Suzanne:	They said it was all right but I knew it wasn't, I knew it could have been much better.
Coach:	So it was good enough for them, but not good enough for you.
Suzanne:	Yeah, but good enough is not good enough for me.
Coach:	How could you get this done in a way that was not only good enough for them, but also enabled you to feel ok about it?

Suzanne: I don't know. Part of me would have to tell myself that it is not my fault that they want this done without giving me enough time to do it, and another part of me would have to say 'OK I'll just get this done,' but nine out of ten times I am going to make sure that when I do some work for them it's up to my standards not theirs. If they don't let me do that, I'm going to look for another job.

The context for Suzanne's issue is a busy, pressurised work environment where staff are constantly having to meet deadlines.

Suzanne has certain standards for her own performance (we don't know at this stage whether these are realistic or not), which are often higher than those expected by her manager. This creates tension and frustration on both sides. In this short piece of dialogue the coach avoids an either/or position (Suzanne's right and the manager is wrong or vice-versa), and instead offers a both/and scenario. How could she maintain her own standards and also meet the demands of her manager? This compromise position enables her to accept that sometimes she will have to hand in work she is not entirely happy with, but will be able to rationalise these as long as they do not happen too often. The coach may also highlight that she has the useful skill of being able to produce a fast turn-around at an acceptable standard. The original dilemma has been re-negotiated in a way that might lead to a satisfactory outcome for both sides.

Building a foundation of competence

Opening moves

Life is one big experiment and starting on a life-project rarely comes with a guarantee of success. There is always the risk of failure. Unless we accept and live with the possibility of failure we are unlikely to ever succeed. A solution focused coach will encourage a coachee to 'make a start and see what happens.' Too often people think they need to have worked everything out before they begin. Some people want to control every detail of a project and when they find they can't, the project either never gets off the ground or fails. Once you start on a project or goal, things happen.

Making a beginning creates a space for something different to emerge. Energy follows action. It is useful to have clear goals as long as they are not rigid or prematurely set. We need the flexibility to change our strategies in the light of emerging situations.

The opening moves in a coaching relationship are crucial because they signal the way in which the two parties will collaborate. For example, a solution focused coach is unlikely to begin a meeting with, 'How can I be helpful?' because this implies that the coach will do expert-like things to or for the coachee. Since solution focused coaching aims to be coachee-centred and to put the coachee's expertise centre stage, this would not be a helpful opening message. Faults in the early set-up of a meeting can have significant negative consequences for the rest of the work.

Once the introductions are over, the coach will ask an *outcome* question such as:

- How will you know that this meeting has been useful to you?
- What do you hope to take away from this meeting?

And a *process* question such as:

- What needs to happen here today for this to be worth-while for you?
- What do you need to do and what do I need to do?

Taking time to explore the answers to these questions pays off in the long run. It ensures that the relationship gets off on the right foot with minimal misunderstandings. It enables both parties to negotiate how they will work together. Solution focused coaches, like most coaches, explain how they work and what the coachee can expect. A typical brief explanation may be along these lines:

Being solution focused means that I will ask you questions about what is already working for you and how you can do more of it. I hope to help you to be more aware of your strengths and skills and how you can apply them to reach your goals. I will not impose solutions or advice, unless you ask me to share my ideas as to what might help. If you do, I will encourage you to adapt them to your situation. I will do my best to help you reach your goals and I am confident that you will also do your best.

In print this may sound somewhat stilted, but in practice the coach delivers it in a warm, friendly, positive tone that conveys interest in and enthusiasm for working with the coachee.

Solution focused coaching language

Solution focused coaches help coachees to achieve their goals by raising their awareness of their skills, strengths and pre-existing solutions. They draw out what's already 'there' rather than put in what is not. They challenge and empower coachees to imagine and use solutions that will work for them. In our experience, the clarity and simplicity of solution focused language motivates people to work towards their goals.

An observer of a solution focused coaching meeting would hear the coach:

- Set the context for the meeting.
- Acknowledge the coachee's issues.
- Restrict any theorising about the 'causes' of a problem.
- Show curiosity about the coachee's abilities.
- Use 'how, when, what' questions but rarely 'why'.
- Challenge supportively any defeatist, self-destructive talk
- Enquire about 'exceptions' – times when the coachee manages situations better.
- Encourage the coachee to keep doing what works and if it isn't working, to 'do something different'.
- Give positive feedback about the coachee's skills and qualities.

The art of listening

An observer may be surprised to see how much listening the SF coach does, as a common misunderstanding of the approach is that it pushes coachees towards solutions from the very beginning of a meeting. This would be more solution forced (Nylund and Corsiglia, 1994) than solution focused. What we listen for and how we listen is dependent upon the model of coaching being followed. A person-centred coach may believe that listening, clarifying and summarising interventions are what is needed to bring about change. Some models will emphasise the importance of listening and drawing out coachees' feelings. A cognitive model will target the coachee's beliefs about themselves in the world.

Listening is a complex activity and can have different purposes. The following is not an exhaustive list:

- We can act as a sounding board for people to test out their ideas and experiences.
- We can listen in order to build rapport in the hope of influencing the other person.
- We can listen in order to comfort or rescue the other person from their distress.
- We can listen in order to agree with the other and by so doing curry favour with them.
- We can listen in order to assess the situation and identify need.
- We can apparently listen, but actually be only waiting for a pause so that we can talk, as we think that what we have to say is far more interesting than what the other person is saying.

Reflection

In addition to listening and questioning, the coach reflects back to the coachee the key elements of their responses. Reflection is not a simple summary (which can become tedious), it consists of two elements; reflect back and nudge towards solutions.

The first part of the response connects with what the coachee has just said and the second part adds a goal-oriented statement.

Example

Coachee: I feel pulled in two different directions, I'm confused.

Coach: You feel confused and you'd like to sort out which
              way to go with this.
Coachee: I wish it was simpler, it sounds too complicated.
Coach: So it would be helpful if we could try to keep it
              simple and not get bogged down in the detail. If
              you had to put into two sentences what you are
              trying to achieve, what would you say?

The coach often, but not always, takes the last thing the
coachee says and uses that as the first part of his response.
Matching the coachee's language helps the coach stay close
to the coachee's meaning.

Silence

Silence encourages coachees to think for themselves. It is
often easier for the coach to advise, guide and tell than it is
to ask, facilitate and support. It can be tempting to take on
the role of the 'wise person' who knows best. But in the long
run the coach who allows space is enabling the coachee to
develop skills for life – skills for making decisions, skills for
analysing and judging situations, skills for utilising their
talents. Doing so shows respect for coachees' knowledge,
skills and life experience.

Asking coachees, 'What do *you* think?' is, in my experience, of greater value than coaches always saying what *they*
think. There is a place for this, but if overdone it becomes
counter-productive and is at the expense of helping coachees
to work it out for themselves. Skilled coaches know the right
amount of 'stretch' for their coachees – who benefits from
robust challenging, who needs more support at this time,
who acts upon advice and who needs to find out things for
themselves.

Powerful questions

An observer would notice that the coach primarily asks
questions to which only the coachee knows the answers. The
purpose in asking questions is not to help the coach collect
information about any problems, but for the coachee to

collect evidence about their solutions. Their solutions are often 'signature solutions' – unique ways of handling difficulties that have worked well for them over a long period of time. Solution focused coaches invite their coachees to reflect upon these patterns so that they can re-activate them when needed. Enabling coachees to do this requires that the coaches stand back and not interrupt this search for solutions. Doing less in this instance is a way of doing more.

It is important that coaches do not over-do questions, otherwise it can feel like an interrogation. There is a skill in knowing when to push and when to back off. Experienced and skilled coaches are able to deliver powerful questions at the right time. These questions will often not have been asked before and may come as a surprise to the coachee. They can provide pivotal moments when coachees have a 'light bulb' moment that illuminates their thinking.

A solution focused coach asks a wide range of questions. These will be considered here according to the SOLUTION coaching model presented in Chapter Two.

1 Share updates

When coachees make a first appointment they will be asked

> It would be helpful if between now and the time you come for your appointment, you could notice any changes which take place.

Early on in the first meeting the coach will invite the coachee to talk through any pre-meeting change by asking whether there have been any changes. We know from therapy that a high percentage of clients (62 per cent) make constructive changes in the interval before they come (Lawson, 1994). Interestingly, researchers found that if the question was asked in a way that implied that the client *wouldn't* have made any positive changes, 67 per cent agreed they hadn't. This is another example of how crucial the interviewer's tone of voice and facial expression are in determining the responses they receive.

Coachees may also make positive changes because they focus on the issue knowing they are going to be asked about it when they come. Having a 'reporting' session coming up tends to encourage people to move their issue higher up the agenda. What is particularly useful about pre-meeting change is that any progress made can only be credited to the coachee, not the coach. When the coach reports any positive changes the coach will ask, 'How did that happen? What did you do?' In this way maximum learning can be extracted from the evidence. By highlighting coachee competence at the beginning of the session, the coach is setting the tone for the rest of the work together. It reinforces the solution focused principle of 'building on what you *can* do.' Pre-meeting change enables the coachee to 'hit the ground running.' Positive pre-session change is a good predictor of a successful outcome (Beybach *et al.*, 1996).

2 Observe interests

Solution focused coaches initiate 'problem-free talk' by inviting coachees to talk about how they spend any leisure time they have. These conversations often help a coach to know:

a) How to engage best with the coachee.
b) Which examples or illustrations will resonate with them.
c) The range of their strengths and qualities.

This opening to the meeting may surprise a coachee who is expecting to focus immediately upon their issues. This initial conversation is not merely small talk or an ice-breaker. It often reveals aspects of the coachee's personality, which can be helpfully incorporated into the proposed solutions. Sometimes it is clear that a coachee needs to reclaim neglected interests and activities in order to build a platform for progress.

Example

Problem-free talk with Anna focused on how she used to enjoy running. What she enjoyed most about it was that while running she completely switched off from thinking about work. She also enjoyed the solitariness of it, as she spent all day in a busy, open-plan, noisy office. Her running was a great antidote to stress. However, she had become so busy at work that she had not managed to fit in any runs. As she talked about it she realised how important it was to her and how much she missed it. She decided that she needed to change her schedule to ensure that she fitted in at least two runs a week.

What the coach learned about Anna was:

a) She renews her energy by having times of quiet on her own. Some of us draw energy from interactions with others and some of us by being on our own.
b) Physical activity helps her to achieve a balance in her life.
c) She likes a challenge, as there had been times in the past when she pushed herself to run when she didn't feel like it.
d) She needs to be careful that she doesn't turn even her leisure pursuits into goal-driven stressful events.

3 Hopes and goals

This step involves listening to problem-talk (what's happening now) and, when the coachee is ready, shifting the focus to the future by exploring the coachee's hopes, aspirations and goals (what they would like to happen).

Whilst listening to problem-talk, questions and probes might include:

- Tell me more about that.
- I can see this is important to you.
- From what you say this is causing you much concern, and it is important to you to address this.

Goal exploration questions might include:

- What would you like to change?
- If you were to make some changes soon, what would be most helpful to you to start with?
- What would you like to stop doing? What would you like to start doing?
- What do you see as your goal?

- How will you know when you have successfully changed the situation?
- What does the future look like without the problem?
- What are your best hopes for this coaching session?
- What would you like to achieve today, for this coaching session to have been worthwhile?
- How will you know when things are beginning to get better for you?
- What helped you to decide that you were ready for this?
- On a scale of zero to ten, with ten meaning that you would do everything you could to achieve your goal and zero being hardly anything, where would you put yourself today?
- How confident are you that you can achieve your goal?
- How do you know this?
- What would other people say that would encourage you?
- What will be the benefits for you in achieving your goal?
- Will there be any benefits for other people?
- Knowing yourself, what needs to happen to get you started?

4 Understand exceptions

Solution focused coaches encourage coachees to switch the focus of their attention from 'seeing' mainly problems, to noticing when, and how, constructive and positive events happen in their lives. They can choose to see half empty or half full glasses for example. They can choose to dwell on a mistake they made, or they can study how they were successful on other occasions. The more coachees become 'solution-sensitive,' the more they become aware of solutions that are available to them. We believe that it is more productive for coachees to notice when they are at their best; to recognise and remember what they are doing right. How were they thinking at the time? What were they saying to themselves? Who were they with? What did they do that was different? We call these occasions 'exceptions' to the problem.

Obviously, the more there are of them, the less predominant the problem. These exceptions are always present because we do not reproduce any behaviour in exactly the same way every time. We are always changing. We have good days and bad days, we're up, we're down, we're full of energy, we're lethargic. Variations in behaviour allow us to explore times when things were better and how they came about.

The coach listens carefully for phrases that imply that exceptions have taken place. These include:

Most of the time	Quite often
Normally	Sometimes
At the moment	So far
It's up and down	Not so bad

These all imply fluid situations. Change is constant and inevitable. Stability is an illusion. There are always occasions when coachees handled situations better. In sports psychology the holy grail of 'exceptions' is when the sportsperson gets 'into the zone.' These are times when the competitor is fully in the moment, free from external influences, unencumbered by thoughts of any kind. This state of detached, deep relaxation frees the non-conscious mind to take over. (We tend to avoid using Freudian terms such as 'subconscious.')

Many people are very aware of their weaknesses and failings. Their failures or mistakes are deeply imbedded in their memories. These memories come with powerful emotions attached. We tend to remember criticism more than praise. We particularly remember bad times, unless we make deliberate efforts to block them out. Many sports people are adept at blocking out their failures in order to minimise the effect on their future performance. There may well be some wisdom in this, as the more we think and talk about something the bigger it is likely to become.

Example

Ben finds it very stressful to have workmen in the house.

Ben: I hate having workmen in the house. They really stress me out and I get very anxious because I feel stupid when they ask me questions that reveal how ignorant I am of all things practical.

Coach: Is it always like that or do you handle it better sometimes?

Ben: I have to work really hard not to get anxious and I'm always glad to see the back of them.

Coach: What do you mean by working really hard? What do you do that helps?

Ben: I tell myself that I'm good at what I do and that I have no ambition to be a builder or an electrician or whatever. I make it clear that I expect them to come up with solutions to problems, just as I do in my work.

Coach: So you remind yourself about your own skills and competence. What else do you do?

Ben: I make some rules with them at the beginning about when they will start and finish each day. It helps if I know they will be going say by 5.30pm and I have time to recover.

Coach: Anything else?

Ben: I had a couple of bad experiences with some workmen who were really arrogant and thought-less. Now I am a lot more careful about whom I employ. If I feel at all uncomfortable with them when they come to quote for the job, I don't take them on.

Coach: Would anyone have noticed anything different about you when you were handling these situations better?

Ben: Definitely. They would have noticed I was more relaxed and that I was taking a more laid back attitude to it all.

Coachees can train themselves to be more perceptive about these occasions.

Many of the questions used by the coach assume skills that are essential for the coachee to make progress.

Question	Assumes Skills
How did you do that? ⟶	behavioural
What difference did that make? ⟶	observational

What did you learn from that? ⟶	learning
What helped? ⟶	self-awareness
What else? ⟶	thinking
What might you do differently ⟶ next time?	applied learning

How did you do that? This implies that coachees used certain skills to achieve a result. These skills may be in the area of behaviour or in thinking; for example, they changed their attitude towards the situation. They 'changed the viewing, then changed the doing.'

What difference did that make? This encourages coachees to notice the impact of their actions, not only for themselves but for others.

What did you learn from that? This emphasises that for progress to take place we need to learn from our experiences. If we made a mistake or failed in some way we need to be encouraged by how we corrected or recovered from it. If it is a success, we need to know how we achieved it so that we can be successful again.

What helped? This invites coachees to identify what specifically worked for them. What was the difference that made the difference? If we can find and remember the answer to that question, we are on the way to building upon our achievements.

What else? This is a key solution focused question because it enables the coachees to look for more helpful evidence directly related to their solutions.

- What else did you do that was helpful?
- What else did you do that was different?
- What else do you know that could be useful to you?
- What else have you tried in the past that it might be worth trying again?
- What else do you think you could do to stop the problem getting worse?
- What else do you know about yourself that will help you to meet this challenge?

'What else?' encourages the coachee to dig deeper for insights which will lead to positive outcomes. This search for solutions may feel like hard work to the coachee, but brings far greater success than accepting someone else's solutions. It respects the coachees' unique and transforming experiences.

5 Tap potential

Solution focused listening builds rapport and raises coachee awareness of their strengths, qualities and skills. This competence-awareness is the foundation for future progress. Helping coachees to have a realistic ownership of their skills and strategies is the first step. This reality-check will hopefully give them the confidence to take the next step forward. Some coachees will have low self-esteem and tend to minimise their strengths, while others may have an unrealistically high opinion of their abilities. The skilled coach encourages the former and tries to contain the latter! Listening carefully for any real evidence of their coachees' strengths does not mean that coaches are unaware of their weaknesses. In the workplace the person that decides whether the coachee is competent will not normally be the coachee him or herself. There will usually be performance indicators to measure competence. In these circumstances the coach will need to be aware of this information and work with it.

A key coaching skill is sensing the right time to raise coachees' awareness of their competence and skills. If done badly it can come across as patronising. If done well, it can give coachees a new perspective on themselves and their situation.

Example

Catherine:	I am finding it hard to get on with a colleague at work.
Coach:	So what's happening?
Catherine:	I get very angry because she's just lazy and I get landed with a lot of work that she should be doing.
Coach:	So how are you handling it at the moment?
Catherine:	I've tried to have a reasonable conversation with her, but she just keeps telling me that I'm out of order and exaggerating.

Coach: How do you react to that?
Catherine: I've got near to losing my rag at times.
Coach: Near to but you didn't?
Catherine: I had to get out of the office on one occasion, she was really doing my head in.
Coach: So although this situation is causing you a lot of annoyance, you decided that losing your temper wouldn't help and you've taken steps to cool off when necessary.
Catherine: It wasn't easy I can tell you.
Coach: I can imagine, how did you do it?

The coach reflects Catherine's story back to her, while highlighting her awareness and skills in controlling her emotions. The 'How did you do it?' question invites her to think further about what she has already done to handle this situation. This is only the beginning of the meeting, but the coach is already laying down a competence marker. Supportive, yet challenging questions will be one of the main forms of intervention the coach will use.

Here are some additional example questions that might be used to help the coachee raise self-awareness and identify resources.

To increase self-awareness:

- What does it say about you that you managed to do that (when coachee has achieved something)?
- Did you know you could do that?
- Where did you learn to do that? Have you done it before?
- Has anyone else noticed that you have done this?
- Who was most surprised that you did it?
- Who was least surprised?

To tap resources:

- Thinking of a recent success you've had, what skills/qualities did you use to make it happen?
- Who and what did you find helpful or unhelpful?
- What is your greatest strength when it comes to tackling challenges?
- What have you learned about yourself that will stand you in good stead in this situation?

6 Imagine success

Although we can learn from our histories we are also deeply influenced by our anticipation of the future. Our predictions shape our behaviour, thinking and feelings in the present. Some coachees may be stuck in the past, perhaps remembered as a 'golden age' or as a time of disappointment and disillusionment. Those who spend their time 'looking forward to the past' are likely to have problems envisaging a successful future. Some may take a fatalistic attitude, having tried for a long time without success to achieve their goals. Their history of failure makes it difficult for them to imagine that their future will be any different from their past. In my experience, solution focused questions help to overcome the negative, fatalistic and self-defeating thinking of some coachees.

Solution focused coaches employ a range of 'preferred future' questions. These questions direct the coachee's attention away from a pre-occupation with history, problems, deficits or difficulties and divert their energy into solution-construction. They invite the coachees to use their imagination to visualise what will be different in their lives when things go well. Their responses help to clarify their goals and strategies. One form of the preferred future question is the Miracle Question (de Shazer, 1988). Its standard form is:

> Imagine one night when you are asleep, a miracle
> happens and the issues we've been discussing disappear.
> As you were asleep, you didn't know that a miracle had
> happened. When you wake up what will be the first signs
> for you that a miracle has happened?

It is as if the person's life had fast-forwarded when they were asleep and when they woke up they had achieved their goals. This is very different from asking someone how they could get from where they are to where they would like to be. Such a question may well lead to a focus on the difficulties of achieving the goal. In the miracle scenario however, the coachee has already arrived at the destination. The Miracle Question assumes that the goal is achievable and that somehow something has changed to make it so. The significant question therefore is what change did this 'miracle' include that enabled you to make a difference? In the ensuing discussion the coach will talk with the coachee not only about how the changes happened but how they impacted on other people. How did they react when they noticed the change? What did they do or say? How did that affect the coachee? As coachees explore their new scenario the hope is that they will realise what practical steps they need to take to achieve their goals.

Sometimes the responses to these questions reveal previously unmentioned problems. Some coachees recall negative past experiences. Others realise that they do not want what they thought they wanted. Whether the responses to the questions are negative or positive they can be revealing and helpful.

The Miracle Question (de Shazer, 1988) works best when the coach takes his or her time and asks it quietly and supportively, with pauses between the phrases to allow the coachee to express their thoughts. Where appropriate, the coach may invite the coachee to use her senses to imagine her daily life without the problem – what would she see/taste/hear/touch/smell when these changes happened?

It is important to emphasise that the 'miracle' has happened to the coachee, not to other people or to the organisation or wider society.

Similarly the description of the preferred future should remain within the boundaries of reality and not be a statement of unrealistic wishful thinking. It is helpful if the coach encourages the coachee to describe the presence of positive behaviours, rather than the absence of negatives e.g. 'I would be calm and relaxed,' rather than 'I wouldn't be so stressed.'

Example

Jack is an inveterate procrastinator. He only manages to perform a task when faced with an immovable deadline and a threat of sanctions. This cliff-hanging lifestyle gets him through most of the time, but he comes unstuck on occasions when he misses a deadline.

Coach: I've got an interesting question for you Jack, which many people find helpful. I'd like you to imagine that you're at home asleep. While you're asleep something amazing happens – you develop the art of meeting deadlines with ease. But because you're asleep you don't know this has happened, so when you wake up and start your day, what will be the first thing that will tell you that you have a new more useful style of working?

Jack: I'd be getting out of the door in time for work.

Coach: What would you be doing differently?

Jack: I wouldn't be wasting time on the Internet instead of getting ready to go out.

Coach: So if you weren't wasting time on the Internet, what would you be doing instead?

Jack: I'd be more focused on what I was doing and what the time was.

Coach: How would you be doing that?

Jack: As I say, I'd keep away from the laptop and just concentrate on doing what I need to do to get out on time.

Coach: What about when you get to work, what would you notice there?

Jack: I wouldn't be so easily distracted.

Coach: What in your opinion distracts you most?

Jack: Emails. I'm always checking them and replying right away when I don't need to.

Coach: So what would you be doing differently to give you a chance of keeping your focus on what you need to do?

Jack: I'd be checking them less often, instead of reading all of them as soon as they come in and then replying to some of them, even when they're not important or urgent.

Coach: In this new scenario will you have a skill you didn't have before?

Jack: Yeah. I think it would give me a system for dealing with emails. I need to discipline myself to open them maybe only three or four times a day.

Coach: When would those times be?

Jack: When I get in, just before lunchtime and say an hour or so before it's time to finish.

The above dialogue is a typical segment of a future-focused conversation. It often centres around one or two specific signs of progress which epitomise the changes the coachee needs to make. Exploring these changes in some depth is the starting point for developing a step-by-step plan, which can be continually updated. The conversation moves in and out of reality, using the imaginative elements to highlight what needs to happen in the real world.

Silence is an important part of the conversation, not only in exploring the preferred future but throughout the meeting. Silence allows for reflection and learning on the part of the coachee and the coach. Sharing the silence supportively can be a powerful and productive experience. Some coaches may feel that they need to be either talking themselves or listening to their coachees talking. Some may think that they need to come up with ideas and questions in order to establish their credibility and usefulness. Some may find silences awkward and rush to fill them. This would be a mistake.

Using the term 'miracle' is inappropriate with some coachees who give it a religious connotation that they are unhappy about. Instead of 'locking horns' with coachees it is far better to use alternative future-focused questions instead.

Alternative future-focused questions include:

- Imagine one night when you are asleep, something amazing happens and the problems that have been worrying you disappear. Since you are asleep you don't know that this has happened. When you wake up in the morning and go about your day, what will be the first signs for you that things have got better?
- Do you think that any of these things have happened to you recently, even for a short while?
- If I were to meet you in a few months' time and you were to tell me that things were getting better, what would you tell me had happened?
- If you were aiming to bring about change in this area of your life, what would be the first sign for you that you were making progress?

- If you went home/into work/to the meeting tomorrow and things had somehow got better, what specifically would you notice that was different?
- If say you were one on the scale with this today and when you came to it tomorrow you realised you were two or three, what would tell you that you had moved up the scale?

7 Own outcomes

The intention at this stage is to clarify the steps to be taken, to explore the coachee's confidence in taking these actions and to prepare them for coping with any setbacks that might arise.

Questions that might be useful include:

Clarifying next steps

- What small steps might you take? What is the first step to be taken?
- What have you tried so far that you know does *not* work?
- Is it time to do something different?
- Do you know anything that has worked for someone else in a similar situation?
- How would you advise a friend who was having this problem?
- What is the smallest step you could take in the next 48 hours that would be helpful?

Exploring confidence

- On a scale of one to ten, where ten is completely confident, how confident do you feel? If less than seven, what might you consider changing to make you feel more confident?
- What do you think you need to do/think/remember to keep your solution on track?
- How will you encourage yourself if you have a set back?
- What will be the best way of handling a set back?
- What will be helpful/unhelpful?
- How will other people know that you need help at that point?

- How will you overcome any obstacles that get in the way?
- If it isn't helpful enough, what's plan B?

One of the reasons the coachee may be having problems is that he or she is rushing from one failed solution to another, or they try harder doing something that has not worked previously. It is always tempting to think that we must be doing something – anything – to resolve a problem. Yet the wise thing might be to wait, be patient and observe ourselves attentively until the situation begins to change. Changing one piece of behaviour or solving a particular problem without supporting it with a lifestyle change is likely to be a short-lived success.

8 Note contributions

This step is about drawing the session to a close, and represents an opportunity to offer and invite appreciative feedback.

Ending sessions

Solution focused coaching is most often brief and intensive. Typically there may only be four or five sessions. Some solution focused coaches encourage coachees to take responsibility for the ending of a session. They ask them to evaluate how helpful it had been and to summarise what they had learned from it and be invited to draw up a course of action. Other coaches prefer to lead and control the ending in order to ensure that the coachees do not raise supplementary issues and that the session ends on time on a clear, simple and positive note.

A typical closing sequence would be

Give positive feedback about the session
↓
Highlight two or three achievements
↓
Link to goals
↓
Summarise assignment/s

Giving positive feedback

Feedback can strongly influence future performance. In research described by Segerstrom (2006) participants who performed badly on an initial assignment and were told that the next assignment required different skills, worked 20 per cent longer. If they were told that the next assignment required the opposite skills from the first they worked for 50 per cent longer. If they had succeeded in the first assignment and were told that this was a good predictor for their performance on the next one, they worked for 40 per cent longer than those who had performed badly on the first assignment.

Before giving the feedback the coach usually takes a short break of a minute or two to compose 'the message.' He or she introduces the break:

> We're coming to the end for today, but before we finish
> I'd like to think for a minute about what you have said
> today and then give you some feedback.

It helps if this is delivered in a warm, friendly manner which raises the coachee's expectation that the feedback will be welcome and useful! The silent break serves to contain what has happened in the session and allows both parties to reflect on what needs to happen next. The hiatus confers a greater importance to the feedback than may otherwise have been the case.

The coach may look briefly at any notes that have been taken.

The first part of the coach's feedback focuses on the quality of the coachee's participation in the session. The coach will typically use opening phrases such as:

* I was impressed today by the way that you . . .
* I really appreciated how you . . .
* I was struck by . . .

The feedback highlights the positive contributions the coachee made to the session. It could be the honesty/courage/determination/enthusiasm or any other quality he/she displayed. It has to be grounded in what actually happened in the session. This part of the feedback may only last for thirty seconds or so, but it provides an important platform for what is to come later. It goes without saying that positive feedback has to be genuine and is not the coach just 'being nice.' Receiving positive recognition will motivate many coachees, but only if they recognise themselves in the feedback. Some may be embarrassed if paid compliments too directly. Throughout the feedback the coach observes the coachee's body language to see how he/she is reacting and if necessary will fine-tune the delivery.

Highlight two or three achievements

In the next phase the coach recalls two or three specific strategies already working for the coachee that have emerged in the meeting. They could be exceptions or occasions when he/she was higher on the scale. They may be actions the coachee has done to stop the situation deteriorating. The coach encourages the coachee to keep doing what is already working. By linking two or three examples together, the coach may reveal a regular solution pattern. Where there is a pattern of solutions the coach may suggest that this is an enduring characteristic of the coachee, for example, 'The fact that you managed to do X, although it was challenging, suggests that you are not someone who gives up easily.' The following is a typical piece of feedback.

Coach: I thought what you did on Wednesday was impressive. You were feeling tired and stressed, yet you managed to make those difficult phone calls and to go to that meeting which you knew was going to be unpleasant. And on Friday, even though you'd had a difficult week you stayed calm and assertive when your manager made those unreasonable demands upon you. What strikes me is that even when you are not at your best, you show a lot of personal strengths.

Link to goals

Where appropriate, the coach makes a bridging statement linking the coachee's achievements (and the qualities they demonstrated) to the agreed goals.

Coach: What you achieved last week shows how resourceful and determined you are. You're going to find that determination valuable when you're running your own business.

Further example questions or statements that may be useful when reflecting back progress made and noting positive contributions from the coachee during the session are as follows:

- Reflecting on the session, I think you have made great progress towards achieving your goals.
- The skills you employ in sailing will be of great use to you here, for example you said you centre yourself in tense situations to remain calm – this is a real strength of yours.
- You spoke with real clarity on your goal and expressed your motivation to take the next step to achieving it.
- You identified three key exceptions that have helped you to clarify some actionable next steps.
- You identified a number of strengths today that you can draw on to take steps towards achieving your goal: your resourcefulness and natural comfort with networking; your empathy for others and your training in negotiation skills.
- You really embraced the visioning exercises and developed a clear image of your preferred future.
- You have developed a very clear action plan and stated what you want to do as an immediate next step.

Practice tips
- Go slowly at the beginning of meetings in order to ensure a good set-up for the work.
- Pay attention to your use of language – does it lead coachees into exploring problems or possibilities?
- Become curious about coachees' unique sets of skills, strengths and strategies.
- Expand your repertoire of questions and know their purpose.

- Build your confidence in using imaginative, future-focused interventions.
- Spend 80 per cent of the time building solutions and 20 per cent acknowledging problems.
- If possible describe the desired outcome at the beginning of a meeting.
- Use problem-free talk to help coachees find transferable skills.
- Engage in extreme listening!

Discussion points

- Listening is a complex activity and can have different purposes. What are the key aspects of listening we need to be aware of when coaching?
- What are some of the advantages and disadvantages of focusing on exceptions?
- Some solution focused coaches encourage coachees to take responsibility for the ending of a session. What are your views on this approach?
- Feedback can strongly influence future performance. Discuss.

Suggested reading

Berg, I.K. and Szabó, P. (2005) *Brief Coaching for Lasting Solutions.* New York: W.W. Norton.

Grant, A.M. (2006) Solution focused Coaching. In J. Passmore (Ed.) *Excellence in Coaching: The Industry Guide*, pp.73–90. KoganPage: London.

Grant, A. and J. Greene (2001) *Coach Yourself.* Harlow: Pearson Education.

Greene, J. and Grant, A. (2003) *Solution Focused Coaching.* Harlow: Pearson Education.

O'Connell, B. and Palmer, S. (2007) Solution focused Coaching. In S. Palmer and A. Whybrow (Eds) *Handbook of Coaching Psychology: A For Practitioners,* pp.278–292. Hove: Routledge.

Palmer, S., Grant, A. and O'Connell, B. (2007) Solution focused Coaching: Lost and Found. *Coaching at Work*, 2(4): 22–29.

4

More solution focused skills for coaches

Change the viewing change the doing

Thinking errors

Solution focused coaches do not ignore or minimise their coachees' problematic thinking or behaviour. There is always a balance to be struck between support and assisting the coachee to examine their approach. Inevitably there are times when the coach needs to encourage the coachee to examine unhelpful or task-blocking thinking. Some typical unhelpful thinking errors are to:

- Discount positive information and focus exclusively on the negatives e.g. 'My manager's feedback was all negative.'
- Assume rigid all-or-nothing positions, leaving no room for compromise or negotiation e.g. 'If a job's worth doing it's worth doing well otherwise I may as well not start.'
- Refuse to accept any or alternatively take too much responsibility for situations e.g. 'It's all their fault' or 'It's all my fault.'
- Set unrealistic standards by aiming for the unattainable e.g. '100 per cent just won't do.'
- Engage in self-critical talk that saps confidence e.g. 'What's the point.'
- Fail to resist self-limiting automatic thoughts e.g. 'I can't do it. I'm useless.'
- Over-do shoulds, oughts and musts in relation to themselves, other people or organisations e.g. 'I really must perform well' or 'The team must achieve its targets.'

Many problems are caused by the way we appraise situations, particularly under stress ('I can't think straight'). According to informational processing theory (see Beck, 1991; Beck and Clark, 1997), pressured situations triggering stress will tend to polarise our thinking so that it becomes more rigid and less flexible and realistic. As coaches we encourage coachees to develop helpful, flexible thinking habits; to acquire the mental strength and resilience needed to deal with not only a specific issue, but future challenges. Solution focused thinking is a philosophy for life.

The aim is to facilitate a fundamental shift in perception so that coachees raise their awareness of themselves and others and pay more attention to what is already working in their lives and how they could do more of it. The aim is for them to develop robust thinking patterns, which counter the undermining influence of negative and destructive beliefs and perceptions. Noticing and understanding interruptions to the pattern of a problem (exceptions) is one of the major perceptual shifts. It helps when there are other people in the coachee's life who can reinforce and maintain this shift, as in the following example.

Coach: So you think you've made a mistake and that it's all down to you. Let's look at your responsibility in this situation.

Coachee: I'm afraid I made a big mistake and then everything went wrong after that.

Coach: If your colleague was here what would he say?

Coachee: He would probably say I'm beating myself up again.

Coach: Why would he say that?

Coachee: He says that I take responsibility for things that have nothing to do with me.

Coach: So there have been times in the past when you've blamed yourself for the whole thing and in the end it turned out that other people had made mistakes too. What difference would it make to you if you said to yourself, 'I've made a mistake and I'm sorry for it and other people made mistakes too'?

Coachee: I'd probably not get so down about it.

Coach: What would you do instead?
Coachee: I'd be miserable for 24 hours, talk to my colleague and then get over it.
Coach: So how are you going to do this?
Coachee: I need to be clear as to what exactly I did and what other people chose to do and whether I need to apologise for my part.
Coach: Sounds like a good idea to me.

Palmer and Strickland (adapted, 1996) summarise the thinking skills coaches can use to help coachees modify their thinking:

• When things are not going well, observe what thinking errors they are making and note them down.

Frequently these errors will be unfounded assumptions. Assumptions may lead to false conclusions and unhelpful feelings such as anxiety and behaviours.

• Modify their language around the situation. For example, instead of describing an event as, 'My worst nightmare' (extreme thinking), the coachee can tell him/herself 'It's inconvenient, it's a setback, but not a nightmare.' The coachee may use scaling to put things into perspective.

Coach: On a scale of one to ten with ten being your worst nightmare and one being 'this is irritating, but it'll all be forgotten in a few days,' where would you put this situation?
Coachee: It's probably about a four.
Coach: Think about your reaction to it. If ten was 'I'm responding with everything I've got because it is an urgent emergency' and one was you were very laid back about it, where would you put yourself today?
Coachee: I'd say about a seven.
Coach: So the situation is a four and deserves a four response, but you're giving it a seven. What would four look like, what would you be doing or not doing instead?

• Broaden their evidence base. Thinking errors may be due to insufficient evidence. The coachee is only seeing one small part of the picture. Who could give you more information or a different way of interpreting what has happened? Who is able or willing to challenge their narrow vision on this? Could they research it on the Internet? Is there a discussion forum/blog/website that would give them another take on this? There are always different ways of viewing things.

- Be wary of attaching labels to themselves or others. There is a tendency to overgeneralise from the specific e.g. 'I've failed by exam therefore I'm a total failure' or 'I've acted stupidly therefore I'm really stupid.' Failing at one or many tasks or projects does not make a person a total failure. One stupid action does not mean that the person is stupid. Solution focused coaches are wary of absolute 'I am' statements, which are invariably unhelpful. Don't identify the problem with the person. We have a saying in SF, 'there's nothing wrong with you that what's right with you can't fix' (source unknown).

- Think more flexibly. 'Shoulds, oughts and musts' applied to self or others can create unnecessary stress. Sometimes 'shoulds, oughts and musts' applied to ourselves are sometimes used to delay action e.g. 'I must do an excellent job,' which triggers anxiety and leads to displacement behaviour to temporarily reduce anxiety such as tidying up files, cleaning the office or study. It is better to modify them to strong preferential and flexible wishes such as, 'It's strongly preferable to do an excellent job but realistically I don't have to.' We can also convert them into free choices, 'You could and you do have a choice.'

The solution focused coach will steer the coachee away from these thinking errors and ask questions that elicit more positive attitudes:

- What do you believe about yourself that will help you sort this out?
- What evidence is there from your past experience that you have the ability and qualities that could help you now?
- What have you been told about yourself by people who really rate you?
- What would you do differently if you believed what you'd been told?

Predictions

When working with coachees who consistently make negative predictions about their future, the solution focused coach may draw upon the following observations.

- A lot of what people worry about never happens. Have you ever had that experience? If so, what did you learn from it? If you haven't yet, could you notice the next time when you anticipate things will be bad and they turn out to be not so bad?
- Often as children we learn that if we worry about something enough then it usually doesn't happen. This can become habit forming. As adults we often forget why as children we learnt to worry. Sometimes we just need to learn to break the habit.
- People frequently surprise themselves. Have you or anyone else been surprised recently at something you did?
- A lot of people find that doing something different and taking a chance pays off. How close are you to trying something new?
- It helps if you know what you want, rather than what you don't want. What would you like to happen in your life?
- Sometimes it helps to think of what you are doing as an experiment; if it doesn't work out you can do something else.
- Most successful people fail lots of times before they succeed. So failure is not a problem, it's a learning curve.

When the coachee is being negative about everything it is usually unhelpful to attempt to convince them about the positives. They are more likely to exaggerate the negatives in order to justify their position. It can be more useful to acknowledge the negativity:

- It makes sense that you should feel like this.
- From where you are sitting it's difficult at the moment to see anything positive in the situation.
- In your opinion what would need to change before you could be hopeful things could get better?

When there is only unremitting gloom the coach asks coping questions:

- It's hard going for you at the moment, how are you coping with it?
- How do you manage with all this going on?
- Despite all these problems, you're still in there fighting, how do you do that?
- It feels to you that you take one step forward and then two steps back. How do you start moving forward after you've had the set back?
- How long do you think this bad patch is going to last; do you see any light at the end of the tunnel?
- How will things turn out if you do 'nothing'?
- Are there any advantages to you or anyone else if you do nothing?
- What will be the first thing that will happen to let you feel the worst is over?
- When you had a difficult time last time what did you notice got you through?

Reframing

Reframing is to give a different meaning to an event or situation in order to make it more solvable. By changing the language around the event we open up possible new understandings and ways of dealing with it. There are always many ways of understanding a situation. We are often aware that we have only heard one side of a story. When we hear the other person's version the event takes a quite different turn. Reframing may be about the coachee or about someone else in their life.

Some common reframes are:

Behaviour – Reframe
Indecision – wise caution
Lazy – laid back/relaxed
Shy – takes time to get to know people
Impulsive – spontaneous
Boring – dependable, consistent

Reframing is a collaborative linguistic negotiation which gives a fresh perspective of an event. For a reframe to be successful it has to be close enough to the coachee's experience and beliefs to be credible. It has to have some appeal, otherwise the intervention can become an argument with the coach trying to impose a 'revision of history' unacceptable to the coachee.

Normalising

Another intervention designed to help coachees change their viewing of a situation is to normalise it. This is not to minimise the person's concerns or to stereotype them, but to acknowledge that it is okay to feel this way and to have these thoughts. They are appropriate to the situation. Someone made redundant for example, could at some stage feel depressed, angry, resentful, anxious and short-tempered. They may blame themselves. These are the reactions of someone who has experienced a shock that has shaken their view of themselves and their world.

The coach may need to reassure them. For example:

'What you are going through is normal. These feelings and thoughts are what you would expect from a healthy person in this situation. I might even be worried about you if you were not having these. They are temporary and hopefully they will pass over time.' Self-help groups have the advantage of reassuring the person even further, 'We were there and had those experiences too, hopefully things will improve. You are not alone.'

Roll with 'resistance'

Resistance is when the coachee rejects the coach's insights or withdraws co-operation in other ways, for example, not speaking. Solution focused coaches will not be offering a lot of their own 'insights,' but some of the time it will be appropriate and helpful that they do. When coachees 'resist' their insights we do not regard this as defensive and hostile, but consider it to be a request from the coachee to change how the session is being run. It could be that the coach has strayed off the coachee's agenda or is going too fast or too slow, is talking too much or too little. Of course the coach may be spot on in his 'insights' and the coachee feels vulnerable and out of her comfort zone and wants to retreat. The coach needs to decide whether to press ahead despite this level of discomfort or to back off and let the coachee re-group. A certain level of unease can promote learning, but too much leads to the person closing down. When there appears to be a loss of momentum or focus the responsible coach asks, 'Is this being helpful? Are we on track?'

Pre-suppositional questions and statements

Solution focused coaches regularly use pre-suppositional questions to help coachees correct negative thinking errors. These questions assume that change is inevitable and that the desired future has been achieved.

- When you've done X what will be the next thing you will do?
- When things have improved what will you be proud that you did?
- What will it be like when you manage to achieve your goal?
- Who will notice when you have achieved your goal?
- Who will be most surprised?

Scaling

Scaling is a simple, yet powerful technique used by solution focused coaches. It is used as a framework to support key solution focused principles and techniques. It can help coachees to:

- Increase their self-understanding.
- Measure progress.
- Set small identifiable goals.
- Self-motivate.
- Become aware of what works for them.
- Focus on solutions.

0
as bad as
it gets

10
the preferred
future

Coaches invite coachees to rate themselves on a scale of zero to ten, where ten represents the goal to be achieved and zero the work hasn't even started. Some coaches omit the zero and use a scale of one to ten as they see their coachees having already got to one by entering the coaching relationship. Scaling is most often used as a subjective rating by the coachee. Sometimes however the coach defines an objective standard for a particular point on the scale; 'When you manage to keep doing X for three days that will be a four. If you do it for one week that will be five.' For example, if an over-confident performer rates herself as an eight, but the coach knows that she is performing poorly in relation to her peers, the coach will challenge her by demonstrating that what *she* considers to be an eight is only a five to her peers.

The actual numbers on the scale do not matter, what matters is the space between the numbers – that is where the potential for movement lies. The coach explores those spaces by asking the coachee a series of questions.

When scaling for motivation for example, a possible sequence of questions may be:

Coach: If ten represents you would do anything within reason to achieve your goal and zero you are not going to make much of an effort, where would you put yourself at the moment?

Such a question needs to be asked non-judgementally. The coachee needs to own the goal and make the commitment.

Coachee: I'd say I'm a six.
Coach: What does that mean for you? Is it enough to get us started?

Coachee: I think I would have to be at least a seven.
Coach: OK, that's helpful. So the first thing we would need to look at is how you could get from six to a seven. How would you know you were a seven?
Coachee: In terms of my weight, I would need to lose six pounds, then I would feel more confident about starting the programme.
Coach: So is that your starting point?

Here is a further list of questions that could be attached to the scale:

- On a scale of zero to ten, with ten representing the best it can be and zero the worst, where would you say you are today?
- In the past, have you ever been higher up the scale? How did that happen?
- Where would you say you were a day or two ago?
- If you've gone down the scale, how did you stop yourself going further down?
- What do you need to do to prevent yourself from going down the scale?
- Would staying where you are on the scale be good enough for now, given all the pressures on you?
- What might sabotage your efforts and how could you stop it?
- Where would you realistically hope to get to in the next few days/weeks?
- If you move up the scale, what will be the signs for you that you have arrived at that point?
- What would need to happen for you to move up one point on the scale in the next few days?
- What do you know about yourself that makes you hopeful that you can achieve what you want in this situation?
- What have you learned from other times in your life that could be useful to you now?
- What skill/quality/strength would be really helpful for you to use at the moment?

Between-session assignments

In order to create momentum and maximise the value of the sessions, coachees need to take action between meetings. The final phase of the feedback is to agree the next steps. Unlike some forms of coaching however, this next step will usually not be coach-directed. Rather it will emerge naturally from the questioning process. So the 'between-session assignment' is not homework assigned by the coach, but the coachee's strategy, designed in collaboration with the coach. If the conversation has been truly solution focused it will have revealed the strengths, resources and strategies the coach needs to implement to achieve the goal.

   The coach will follow solution focused principles in agreeing between-session assignments:

- If it works keep doing it, unless you can think of a better way of doing it.
- If it isn't working, stop doing it if you can and consider what else you could do.
- Do something different.
- If it isn't broken don't fix it, unless you need to do some maintenance on it.

Example

Coach: So one of the things you said that would get you from five to six was being disciplined about your emails and that instead of you responding instantly to them, you would only open them once an hour. This would help you concentrate more on your priorities. Another thing you were interested in having a go at (having seen how useful it was last week), was that you would stop yourself when you were being negative about situations, as you'd become aware that a lot of the time events didn't turn out nearly as badly as you predicted. So those would be two things that you might want to put into practice this week.

Worksheets

Many coachees are keen to start self-coaching and they pick up on the main aspects of solution focused coaching and apply them outside of the coaching session. Sometimes they find it useful to use a worksheet to guide them through the process. Appendix 1 is a solution seeking worksheet which can be completed with the coach's assistance within a coaching session and then used outside the session for self-coaching.

Notice assignments

Solution focused interventions aim to shift coachees' perceptions of their situation. To some extent this is a shift from negative to positive, from half-empty to half-full, but it is more than that. The interventions stimulate coachees to notice what is *already* working in their lives and how they made that happen. Notice assignments are ways of encouraging coachees to process information differently – to reframe their reality in a way that makes movement forward more likely. A notice assignment is often given to coachees who are unable to identify exceptions to their problems, are unclear about their preferred future or have few, if any, ideas as to how they could improve their situation. They may be stuck on Problem Island. It may be given to coachees who have not carried out previously agreed 'between-session' assignments. Rather than give them another assignment, they are invited to notice opportunities when they *could* have done it, without being under pressure to do it. Paradoxically, people often go ahead and do it when they've been told just to notice the opportunity!

Specifically the notice assignment could be about:

a) Times when anything constructive or positive happens.
b) Times when someone else does something they find helpful.
c) Times when the expected problem doesn't materialise or is managed better.
d) Events in their lives which they would like to see continue.

If in future sessions the coachee is able to report observations of this kind, the coach explores them further in the search for resources and solutions.

Coach: So you were going to look out this week for times when things went better with your partner. How did that go?

Coachee: It's interesting isn't it, that you tend to see what you're looking for? I decided I would make an effort on Sunday when we spent quite a lot of time together, to just notice things she does that I really appreciate. I was surprised how many small kind things she does for us all, like she would always ask if we wanted a drink when she was making one. I noticed how patient she was when one of the kids was playing up a bit whereas I would have got really fed up with him. She talked him down. I was struck by how much of her day is taken up with doing things for the family and she had very little time for herself. That was a bit of a shock.

Coach: I just asked you to notice things so I don't expect you did anything about this.

Coachee: Well actually I said to her, 'Come and sit down for a minute, you've been on your feet all day doing things for everyone.'

Coach: How did she take that?

Coachee: I think she really appreciated it. We cuddled up on the sofa and watched TV for half an hour. Maybe I need to help more.

Pretend assignments

A pretend assignment is one in which coachees are invited to act 'as if' the changes they want have already happened. Acting as if you feel confident/relaxed/brave, even for a short while, can help to teach you how to do the real thing. It can also be helpful to visualise yourself in another context or time when you did feel confident/relaxed/brave. What was that like? Is there anything in that situation you could transfer to help you carry off this one? Doing something when your feelings are telling you the opposite is not easy, but it is possible. When an individual acts differently others often respond differently.

'Do something different' assignment

The aim here is to encourage coachees to break with unhelpful routines and to escape from stuck patterns of behaviour. Constantly repeating failed solutions de-motivates and drains the person of their creative energies. The 'something different' (O'Hanlon and Weiner-Davis, 2003) could be to:

a) Change the frequency or rate of doing the problem; for example, frequent small meals eaten very slowly rather than bingeing rarely.
b) Change the timing of the problem behaviour; for example, instead of going to bed at 2 am go at midnight.
c) Change the location where the problem behaviour takes place; for example, going out for a walk when feeling depressed.
d) Change the duration of the problem behaviour – vary time spent surfing the net instead of always putting in a six hour shift.
e) Notice that the problem behaviour does not take place in certain circumstances; for example, someone with a heavy drinking problem cuts down when the grandchildren are around.

'Do something different' is a deliberate attempt to manipulate the social environment in which 'goal sabotaging' has been occurring. Changing the circumstances breaks the 'problem mould.' Doing something different is an experience of power and control. It underlines the fact that even in difficult situations there are always options even if they are limited. The solution focused approach makes people accountable, emphasising their power to shape events and achieve outcomes. It also highlights the need to keep on top of our actions if we are to ensure that we are moving towards our goals.

If the coach is unsure what to ask the coachee to do he might say,

> I'd like to give you an assignment that would help and that you feel pretty confident you could do, any ideas what that would be? It would have to be quite achievable and something you feel ready for.

As Carl Rogers used to say, 'If in doubt ask the client.' The same could apply if a coach is struggling to know what question to ask the coachee:

> I'm not sure whether I'm missing something here and if there is a question it would be helpful I asked you. If you were me what would you ask you now?

Maintaining change

Hopefully, it will be clear by now that coachee self-reliance and resourcefulness lie at the heart of the relationship. The approach consistently privileges the expertise of the coachee over the wisdom of the coach. It does not encourage dependency but always aims for sustainable solutions. Coaches stimulate and support the learning and change processes. However, as we all know, making and maintaining change is not easy. We start with the best of intentions, but we can easily fall back into our default positions. We may discover that other people do not respond in the way we had hoped for. We may feel unsettled by awkward and unfamiliar behaviours. We are creatures of habit! We may begin to doubt whether it's worth the trouble. Our efforts to change may not have produced the payoff we hoped for and there may even be unintended negative consequences. It is tempting to give up and retreat to our comfort zone.

In order to imbed change and maintain momentum, the coach assists the coachee to anticipate obstacles and setbacks and to put in place strategies that will help him or her back on track.

The following questions for endings may help further reflection.

- What makes you confident that you can carry out the plan?
- What do you think will get in the way and how will you deal with it?
- What do you need to remember if you have a set-back?
- If things are not going well, how will you know whether to stick with the plan or to change it?
- What do you know about yourself? Do you tend to stick with plan A come what may? Do you go to plan B too early?
- Who could help you with all of this?
- How will you know we need to meet and talk about it?
- What will make all of this worthwhile?

Sometimes the coachee may block themselves from achieving their goal(s) by not taking personal responsibility. This can be quite subtle. The coach needs to focus on what is within the coachee's sphere of influence. That includes his or her own behaviour, predictions and perceptions about a situation. The coach may need to recall useful data provided by the coachee in a previous session and encourage further reflection as in the following example.

Coach: Today we have discussed how you are going to get on with the project. At our previous meeting you mentioned that you just don't have the time to get some important tasks completed.

Coachee: Yes. I get overloaded with tasks and projects. My manager gives me too much work.

Coach: How could you make the time to complete the important tasks? (The coach placing responsibility back onto the coachee.)

Coachee: I don't know.

Coach: Hmm. I wonder if you have told your manager that you are being given too much work? (Coach focusing on what is within the coachee's sphere of influence and has a hunch that the coachee has not shared work overload issues with his manager.)

Coachee: No, not really.

Coach: Is it worth discussing your current the workload with your manager in order for you to complete the important project? (Encouraging the coachee to talk to his manager is within the coachee's sphere of influence although the outcome may not be.)

Coachee: I suppose so. He may not listen so what's the point.

Coach: So your prediction is that he may not listen. (Coach highlighting it is a prediction and not fact.) I suppose you could put your prediction to the test. Do you have anything to lose if you did?

Coachee: Not really.

Review assignment performance

Solution focused coaches aim to keep coachees focused on solutions as much as possible. So the priority in subsequent sessions is to elicit any evidence for what has worked since last time. This may be the successful completion of the assignment, which helps increase self-efficacy (see Bandura, 1997). Sometimes coachees fail to carry out the assignment, but do something else more relevant and helpful. Depending upon the circumstances, the coach may suggest that the coachee varies the assignment if the situation demands it. Plan A sometimes sounds good at the time but simply does not work out in practice.

When a coachee declines to perform an assignment on more than one occasion then both parties need to:

- Decide whether the goal requires redefining, perhaps it was over-ambitious or inappropriate.
- Re-evaluate the strength of the obstacles in the way and adapt the assignment to overcome them.
- Agree to re-schedule the assignment. Perhaps it was just not a good time to implement the assignment.
- Explore coachee's thinking behind the non-performance, e.g. did it lead to increased anxiety and subsequent procrastination?

- Review the coachee's level of motivation with a possible re-focus on increasing it.
- Consider how much the coachee owned the strategy or how much of it was coach-driven.
- Give no further assignments until the picture is clearer.

The coach will begin any session, other than the first, with a variation of the following question:

What's changed/what's better or what's different?

If the coachee can report any progress the coach will explore this in some detail.

Coach: It's been a couple of weeks since we met, so what's better for you?

Coachee: Pretty much the same really.

Coach: What was the day after the last session like?

Coachee: I saw you on the Monday and on the Tuesday I had to go to a meeting I dread. But actually it wasn't so bad.

Coach: How come, what happened?

Coachee: Normally I keep out of the way as much as possible. I can't stand speaking in public as you know.

Coach: Yes, it's a challenge for you.

Coachee: Well actually I surprised myself, because I spoke up more than once.

Coach: How did you do that?

Coachee: I was really nervous and I could hear my voice shaking.

Coach: You were nervous but you still did it.

Coachee: I was quite pleased with myself because people seemed to take my point seriously and quite a few agreed with me.

Coach: How do you think you did this, because it doesn't come easily to you?

Coachee: I had thought about what I was going to say before the meeting and it was important to me to get my point across. I just took a few deep breaths and did it. Afterwards I was worried about what people might have thought, but a couple of people

came up to me and thanked me for saying what
they had wanted to say but couldn't.

Coach: So how does doing that fit with the goal of building
              your confidence?

Coachee: I felt it was a real breakthrough.

Coach: So what else has been better since last time?

Upbeat interventions are not always appropriate since
coachees often need to talk about their concerns and difficulties since the last meeting. Using the session to learn
from mistakes and failure is as solution focused as learning
from successes.

Ending the relationship

Although there may be a sense of loss at the end of a
successful coaching relationship, there will hopefully be a
sense of achievement and of a job well done. For coachees
there will be an awareness of how much distance they have
travelled and a confidence in their new road map.

Knowing when and how to end the relationship requires
thought and attention (Palmer and McDowall, 2010).
Endings need to be worked towards and ideally there should
be a clear description of what will be happening to indicate
when ending is appropriate. The maintenance questions will
be important in ensuring that the coachee has strategies in
place should problems arise.

Case study

Let us illustrate a range of the skills we have now mentioned
in the previous chapters (see O'Connell and Palmer, 2007:
287–290).

Colin (35) was a team leader in a large company. When
he came for coaching he presented as a genuine, warm,
conscientious and intelligent person. Since his promotion
six months previously, he had come to relish his new role –
managing, supporting colleagues, troubleshooting, generating new ideas, chairing meetings and contributing to the
development of policy.

However, one aspect of his new post caused him a great deal of anxiety – his performance at the monthly senior management meeting. He perceived the atmosphere as pushy and competitive and this intimidated him. For most of the time he kept quiet and hoped to avoid being put on the spot. When he did speak he felt that he was ignored. This experience of being marginalised was affecting his confidence. He felt bullied by some of the powerful members of the group and found it hard to stand his ground. He was beginning to see himself as a failure, letting his own team down by representing them ineffectually to management. When he reported to them that he had failed to raise their issues at the meeting, he felt he was losing credibility as a leader.

He dreaded the management meeting. He would toss and turn in his sleep the night before (often compounded by being disturbed by his two-year-old child). On meeting mornings he felt sick and panicky on the journey to work. He described himself as, 'feeling like a nervous wreck' after these meetings.

When Colin came for coaching the coach acknowledged how difficult these management meetings were for him. Instead of asking for more details of his behaviour at the meetings Colin was surprised to be asked about his strengths as a team leader. In relation to his own team Colin felt that he came across as 'a hard worker, confident, supportive, enthusiastic.' When asked about how friends outside of work would describe him he said, 'loyal, caring, interested in others.' These opening exchanges began to put Colin's situation into context. It was only in the particular circumstances of the management meeting he found it difficult to be himself.

In fact he had many personal and social resources. He was able to describe non-work occasions when he showed that he could be assertive – for example in negotiating with the builders doing an extension on his house. When asked if he had ever had to deal with a similar situation to the one he currently faced at work, he remembered a time in another company when he had to challenge a senior member of staff who was making unreasonable demands of him. He had found that very difficult to do and had to 'psyche himself up' before doing it.

In relation to his resources the coach asked him, 'What quality or strength do you have that would be really helpful if you could use it in the management meeting?' His answer was that he was normally a 'clear communicator.' This led into a discussion about what he does to make his communications clear. In relation to the meeting he thought that he would be communicating clearly when he

- offered his opinion on a subject early in the meeting;
- asked a relevant question;
- presented the team issue;
- kept ownership of his ideas.

Rather than the coach giving Colin tips on how he could do this, he asked him, 'Has there been a time in the meetings when you have done any of this?' The answer was hardly ever, but he did recall one occasion when he backed up a colleague who was under pressure. He had managed to say what he wanted and had kept to this point even when others disagreed. The coach also asked him, 'Is there anything that you are doing in the meeting at the moment that you think it would be helpful to stop doing?' Colin said he could stop engaging in behaviours that put him in a subordinate position – 'I could stop sitting out of the Chairperson's line of vision and stop pouring out the coffee for everyone at the break.'

Using the solution focused intervention known as the Miracle Question (de Shazer, 1988), the coach invited Colin to imagine that something amazing happened when he was asleep one night, a miracle if you like – and this miracle was that he was given the ability to perform well at the next management meeting. As he was asleep at the time he didn't know this had happened. So when he woke up on the day of the next management meeting, how would he begin to find out that something amazing had happened?

In answering this and follow up questions the following picture emerged:

'I would be calmer when I woke up as I would have had a better night's sleep. I'd dress smartly. I would listen to my music on the way to work rather than think about how awful the meeting was going to be. I would have prepared what I was going to say about the team issue. I would remind myself that I am as good as anyone else at the meeting. I'd do some relaxed breathing before going into the meeting. In the meeting I would sit in a position where I can see and be seen. I would say something early on at the meeting – just to make my presence felt. I wouldn't look so worried, I'd be more relaxed.'

Colin's answer to the miracle question led to the development of a plan. He decided to:

- talk to his partner about not having any overnight baby duties the night before the management meeting;
- make better preparation for the meeting – especially by thinking what he was going to say about the team issue;
- take his iPod to work with him;
- change where he sat in the meeting;
- attempt to say something in the meeting early on, even if only to ask a question.

In the feedback at the end of the session the coach reminded Colin about his repertoire of skills as a team leader. He had proved to management that he was promotion material. He had lots of ideas for improving his performance in the management meeting. The coach expressed his confidence in Colin's ability to transfer his skills from one context to another.

When Colin returned for his second coaching session a fortnight later, the focus was on any changes that might have taken place since last they met. Colin reported that he had still felt anxious in the management meeting he had attended, but that he had succeeded in raising his team's issue. The coach was curious as to how Colin had managed to do this. Colin's view was that he had pushed himself to raise it because he kept thinking how disappointed his team would be if he had to tell them he had again failed to do so. He had also felt better going into the meeting because he had managed a good night's sleep previously as the result of having an undisturbed night. He had also carried out his plan to listen to music on the way to work and divert his mind from worrying about the day ahead.

In developing these solutions further the coach asked Colin a scaling question.

Coach: On a scale of zero to ten, with ten being everything is fine and zero really bad, where do you think you are now with the management meeting?

Colin: Three.

Coach: What makes you say three rather than two?

Colin: I think that I have begun to think about it differently. It's not a good meeting for me to think creatively in: it's too competitive. I need to adapt to this and find my own way of handling it.

Coach: So in your view what do you need to do to keep at three or even move to a four?

Colin: One thing I am going to do is to speak to my colleague Emma. She feels the same about the meetings as I do but she seems to have found a way of handling it.

Coach: What else would need to happen for you to get to four?

Colin: Having seen the team's reaction when they heard I got a result for them at the management meeting; that will really keep me going forward.

Further discussion led to Colin formulating his plan for the next step that will move him up the scale. There may be setbacks along the way, but the coach will continue to encourage Colin to play to his strengths, to notice times when he achieves what he wants to achieve and to learn from his experiences. Many of the interventions the coach uses are those that he will encourage Colin to use himself:

- to notice times when he does something positive in the meeting and become aware how he did it;
- to set small goals for himself, which are achievable;
- to use scaling to measure his progress and to identify the next step forward;
- to train himself to use his resources and imagination to devise solutions that work for him.

Over a period of time Colin became more confident and assertive in the management meetings and his stock continued to rise as a team leader. Although attending management meetings continued to be the part of his job he liked the least, he felt that he was doing himself and his team justice.

Practice tips

Don'ts

- Use a lot of 'Why' questions.
- Try to put in what's not there.
- Be the sage on the stage.
- Get into arguments with coachees and 'lock horns'.
- Become attached to your own insights and solutions.

Do's

- Ask 'How' questions.
- Work with what you've got.
- Get out of the coachee's way.
- Be the guide on the side.
- Use pre-suppositional language.
- Scale everything!
- End well.

Discussion points

- Are many problems caused by the way we appraise situations, particularly under stress?
- Why is scaling such a powerful technique?
- How does the 'doing something different' approach work?

Suggested reading

Berg, I.K. and Szabó, P. (2005) *Brief Coaching for Lasting Solutions*. New York: W.W. Norton.

Greene, J. and Grant, A. (2003) *Solution Focused Coaching*. Harlow: Pearson Education.

Palmer, S. and McDowall, A. (2010) *The Coaching Relationship: Putting People First*. Hove: Routledge.

5

The solution focused coach

How you present as a coach is more crucial than your preferred theory or technique. The respect with which you treat the coachee, the quality of your listening and the values that underpin your work are all factors that influence outcome. The skilled coach knows when to speak and when to be silent, when to support and when to challenge, when to ask and when to tell. The coach presents as confident and competent.

A competent coach will be a person of integrity who can communicate warmth, empathy and understanding. A coach requires the ability to do all of the following.

Listen carefully to the coachee without mentally rehearsing the next question or response. It is only when the coachee has finished what he or she wants to say, that the coach then frames her response. There may be a slight pause as the coach reflects upon what has been said before making the next intervention. Since the coach is not listening in order to formulate a hypothesis about the problem, the conversation often appears informal. However, it is also focused and can sometimes be quite intense.

Be non-judgemental. Working with a coachee's unique beliefs, values and strategies, requires the coach to hold a mindset that goes beyond mere acceptance of difference, to one that is willing to learn about the range of attitudes and lifestyles his or her coachees choose. The open-mindedness can come across in the coach's obvious curiosity about the coachee's strengths and solutions. This life-affirming stance on the coach's part creates a safe and containing relationship in which the coachee can explore their hopes and strategies for achieving their goals. The coach requires a disciplined approach to resist the temptation to problem-solve, self-disclose or give advice. Some coaches may think that in order to be credible they need to demonstrate their ability to offer wise and innovative solutions. This is not the case. Coachees trust a coach when they begin to experience insights about themselves and see the difference that solution focused conversations can make.

Be neutral where possible. It's rarely, if ever, helpful for the coach to be more keen than the coachee to reach his or her goal. In situations where the coach has to meet targets to justify her position, there is a danger that the coach will lead from the front and push the coachee into action plans to which he or she is not genuinely committed. It is not helpful for a coach to believe that if they work hard enough they will find an answer for the coachee. A more collaborative stance would be, 'if we work hard enough the coachee can find the answer.'

Use a full repertoire of rapport-building, challenging and solution-construction skills. All three elements need to be kept in balance and applied in different proportions at different times or with different coachees. Inevitably coaches will be stronger in some areas than others. Coachees may enter coaching hoping for a robust, challenging and transforming relationship. A coach who is strong on rapport-building but weak on challenging will not meet their needs. Similarly a coach who has well-developed challenging skills, but lacks the language-craft to draw out solutions will disappoint. The coach needs to be emotionally and strategically intelligent.

Keep out of the coachee's way. Trust the coachee to know what works and don't short-circuit the coachee's own problem-solving mechanisms by introducing coach-initiated solutions. The latter may work for a while, but will not be sustained.

Use the voice to convey a range of emotions. The coach relies upon their voice (supported by body language) to communicate, among other things, enthusiasm, curiosity, challenge, warmth and appreciation. The volume, pitch and tone of voice need to be congruent with the message being conveyed. Matching the coachee's pace and volume of speech is often useful. Appropriate posture reinforces attentiveness – at times leaning forward to communicate interest, at other times sitting back in a more reflective posture as the coach asks the coachee a question. The coach may use their hands to 'draw out' answers from the coachee.The effective coach observes the coachee carefully and modifies his or her voice according to the feedback being received. Overall the coach's body language is relaxed and informal yet conveys genuine interest and support for the coachee.

Ask more than tell. Instead of giving the coachee instructions, the coach will explore the situation in a more personalised way. For example the coach may use this three-step approach with a coachee who has problems in meeting deadlines:

1 How important do you think it is to meet deadlines?
2 What have you found is the best way to meet deadlines?
3 How might you apply this idea to your current deadline?

This gentle, but probing, set of questions draws out ideas based upon what works for the coachee, rather than impose a formulaic strategy that the coachee may have already tried and failed to practise. Solution focused coaches avoid putting their own spin upon their coachees' experiences. They do not presume to know how to fix something that has gone wrong. Instead they help their coachees become more aware of how they have succeeded when they got it 'right.' Trusting the coachee means that the coach takes a pragmatic position that coachees are 'doing their best most of the time.'

Is advice-giving ever appropriate? Yes, but in situations where the coachee fixes the goals it is normally done sparingly. The coach asks the coachee if it would be helpful, 'to put some ideas on the table.' If the coachee welcomes this offer the coach tentatively proposes things they could have a go at, but leaves space for the coachee to fine tune them. Advice has its place but it can be counterproductive. Advice-givers often have their own agenda or base their advice solely upon their own experience. Advice is often ineffective because it does not fit well with the individual's signature solutions. Even when coachees are well-intentioned they find they 'can't do it that way.'

Coach: You sound a bit stuck, would it help if I put a few ideas on the table for you think about?

Coachee: Yes it would, I feel I've tried everything.

Coach: One of the things that strikes me is that you need something different to happen because you are fed up with every day being the same. Your routines are boring you. You could do with a new activity or challenge as long as it is not too time-consuming or difficult.

Coachee: I know but it's hard to think of what to do.

Coach: One way to begin might be by getting more information about what's on in your local area.

Coachee: There's a neighbourhood centre next to the library that has lots of leaflets.

Coach: So maybe one small step would just be to collect some leaflets, look on the notice boards, maybe if you felt like it even talking to one of the workers at the centre. Once you're out there looking, something might happen. At least you've broken the routine.

Coachee: I could pop in when I take the kids to story time at the library.

It's important that the coach does not identify his or herself with any particular solution, otherwise if it is rejected or turns out not to work, the coach may lose credibility. If the coachee does not engage or commit to any action, it is preferable to give them a 'notice' task where they simply observe specific aspects of their situation, without feeling that they need to do anything.

Direct the process. Although the coachee is 'the expert' in his own life, the coach has the expertise to run the meeting effectively. The coach is responsible for crafting the conversation and keeping it moving towards the desired outcome. The coach actively seeks to influence the coachee. To that end the coach may consciously edit and shape the conversation. Some of what the coachee says the coach expands upon, some is acknowledged but not developed, and some is challenged. Some of what is said may be allowed to pass without comment. The coach decides when to go 'deep' and probe to maximise the coachee's learning and when to use a light touch. Depending upon the context, the coachee sets the goals and the agenda, and the coach runs the conversation. But if it takes place in a managerial context, the manager may set non-negotiable goals. This may still leave the coachee free to negotiate the means to achieve the goals.

While being directive of the process, the coach leads from behind. The coach encourages the coachee to lead from the front, to be accountable, to engage with their preferred solutions. It would be contrary to solution focused principles for a coach to manipulate the coachee by steering them towards the coach's preferred solution. There is a transparency about the process. From the beginning the coach will have explained how they work and what their respective roles are. In an organisational setting, if the context requires the manager-coach to set the goal this needs to be made clear from the onset.

Keep focused. The coach regularly connects the flow of the conversation with the desired outcome.

- How does what you've just told me relate to your goal?
- How does what you're planning to do take you nearer to your goal?
- So if you stopped doing that would it be easier to get to where you want?
- If that is still your goal, how can we approach it more positively? Let's look at some of your uncertainties about it.
- If that is where you would like to get to, we need to look at what is taking you in that direction.

While keeping the big picture in view, the coachee needs signposts along the way to encourage and reassure that she or he is heading in the right direction. The solution focused axiom to 'keep it simple' is a warning that detail and complexity can sabotage progress. There is a time for taking the scenic route, but not in coaching meetings. Coaches are also aware that coachees may choose assignments that allow them to remain in their comfort zones, but do not actually address their issues. We all like to do the things we enjoy doing, or stretch us in acceptable ways. We know how to look busy or preoccupied when in fact we are avoiding what we should be doing.

Focused action is relevant to the task in hand and has measurable benefits to the coachee, not necessarily in the short term, but certainly in the long term. In the meeting the coach models the single-mindedness, drive and determination needed by the coachee to attain their goal. Joint completion of coachee's sentences can demonstrate the accuracy and empathy of the coach's listening and understanding (O'Connell, 2005). On occasions the coach can helpfully interrupt the coachee who gets side-tracked or is finding it difficult to distinguish between what is important and what is trivial. Interruptions need to be done courteously, but assertively.

Coach: Could I stop you there? If necessary we could come back to that later. I need to ask you . . . .

Use energising language. Coaching conversations that use clear, specific and pictorial language build momentum towards outcomes. Pemberton (2006) uses the term 'quantum' to describe questions that enable the transition from one energy state to another. 'Why' questions seem to generate a different energy in a meeting from concrete questions such as 'What?' 'Where?' 'When?' and 'How?' It makes a noticeable difference when as a coach you can see 'in your mind's eye' exactly what the coachee is talking about, since that probably means that it is clear to the coachee as well. Hence the value of questions such as:

- What do you need to do right away?
- What needs to happen for you to do that?
- What will you do next?
- When will you know to take the next step?
- What will tell you that you are on the right track?
- How will you know when you have reached seven on the scale?
- How did you know that was a good idea?
- Where could you go to give yourself time to think?

Delivered in a supportive tone of voice these questions challenge coachees to ground their thoughts in concrete action. As has been mentioned before, only the coachee can answer these questions.

Use visualisation. Jeanerod (1983) compared people imagining an action with people actually engaging in these actions and showed that under both conditions the same motor areas became active. Imagining an action and engaging in an action often have the same neuropsychological consequences. Lazarus (1984) developed a number of imagery techniques and exercises that can be used to tackle a range of common problems such as performance anxiety. Libby *et al.* (2007) and her colleagues have demonstrated that it is particularly helpful to visualise yourself performing the desired action *from the point of view of an observer seeing you* (known as external imagery). Ninety per cent of participants in their experiment who had visualised themselves performing the action from a third-party perspective reported that they had gone on to carry out their intended action, compared to 72 per cent who had visualised it from a first-person perspective (internal imagery). The researchers suggest that seeing ourselves as an observer would see us enables us to see ourselves as 'the kind of person' who performs that behaviour, whereas seeing ourselves from a first-person perspective we tend to interpret as saying more about the situation we were in. It could also be that imagining a public performance of an action observed by others gives an additional motivation to do it. Both these pieces of research fit well with the solution focused emphasis on imagining that the preferred future has happened. Describing the 'miracle' from the point of view not of the coachee, but of significant others, may give it additional impact.

- Who will be the first person to notice that the miracle has happened?
- How will they react?
- What do you imagine you will do then?
- What difference to the rest of the day do you think this will make?
- What will your friends/neighbours/colleagues notice?

There may be a caveat. Palmer (2010) reported that within the sports field, internal imagery was found to be more effective than external imagery with experienced sportspeople visualising their sporting activities whereas external imagery was more effective with inexperienced sportspeople. These findings may transfer to personal or executive coaching domains.

Be time-sensitive. Although there is considerable evidence (McDonald, 2007) that the solution focused approach accelerates change and achieves outcomes faster than many other approaches, this does not mean that it is a 'quick fix.' Coachees who want it all sorted more or less instantly, and preferably without much work on their part, are not being realistic. Where for whatever reason there are only a few sessions available, the expectations of the coach and coachee are crucial. If they believe that much can be achieved in a short period of time, then having only a few sessions can help to concentrate minds and target their efforts. It can intensify the experience. If they see coaching as the start of something sustainable, then time limitations need not mean a second-class service. Building rapport quickly; the coach projecting him/herself as competent and confident; keeping close to the agenda and the goals; focusing on what works; the coachee working between meetings – these factors can ensure that time is used with maximum impact. More need not mean better; better means better (Hoyt, 1995). With many coachees who are struggling to raise their performance, overcome barriers or recover optimism and hope, it is important however to 'hurry slowly.' It can take time and tact to uncover the hidden solutions people have forgotten or never knew they had.

Be aware that language shapes realities. The social constructionist philosophy behind the solution focused approach proposes that it is in and through dialogue that the coach and coachee construct meaning. The coachee's 'issues' do not have an objective, fixed meaning that the coachee brings to the meetings. Instead it is through the telling and re-shaping of their story that 'truths' emerge. These truths are only provisional understandings and sometimes misunderstandings! This view of language introduces the idea of flexibility and movement in exploring what the coachee means when he says that he wants to pursue a particular goal or overcome a specific problem. It partly explains the way in which these conversations seem to 'open windows' and allow fresh air to flow into the coachee's life. The coachees then begin to choose ways of understanding their situation that make positive change more possible. As Bertrand Russell once said, 'The greatest challenge to any thinker is stating the problem in a way that will allow a solution.'

Coachee: My problem is that I'm not assertive enough; I let people walk all over me. I can't say no when I'm asked to do something and I get stressed and exhausted as a result.

Coach: So what does it mean for you to be assertive? How will you know you are being assertive enough?

Coachee: I will stand up to some of the bullies at work.

Coach: What will you do when you can?

Coachee: I'd speak up more often when they are saying things that make me feel uncomfortable.

Coach: I know that can be hard, has there ever been a time when you feel you've stood up to them even for a short while?

Coachee: Not really.

Coach: So if I were to see you behaving assertively the way you want to, with one of these difficult people, what would I see happening?

Coachee: I would be standing up and not sitting down with him standing over me. I wouldn't be looking so worried. I wouldn't just be listening, I'd be talking.

Coach: So your body language and energy would be different. Tell me more about that.

Coachee: I'd be standing tall but shoulders down. I'd try to look more relaxed, less tense. Actually as I talk about it, I think I need to pretend I'm more strong and confident than I really feel. Maybe I need to practice looking assertive before I try it at work.

Coach: Is that something you feel committed to doing?

Coachee: Yes, I could practice with a friend of mine who knows about the situation at work.

Coach: So when you have succeeded with this, what will you feel most good about?

Coachee: That I was brave enough to do something that I thought I couldn't do. I think I would like myself more.

Coach: So for you to do this some of the time would change the way you see yourself. What else would you do if you liked yourself more?

Coachee: I would be able to ask for what I need, instead of putting myself at the back of the queue all of the time.

The coach has joined with the client to explore the meaning of the story she tells about herself and to co-create a new and empowering narrative. What coachees often say they value most about these conversations is that they are 'joint productions' uncluttered, practical, clear and respectful.

Become solution-sensitive. By carefully listening with a keen interest in coachee resources, strengths and solutions, the coach hears the possibilities implicit in the coachee's conversation. It is striking how creative and imaginative people are in generating solutions. Human beings show themselves time and again to be resilient, innovative, amazing problem-solvers.

A solution-sensitive coach reads between the lines and responds to any traces of constructive thinking or behaviour. She may use phrases such as:

'From what you've said I'm picking up that you . . .'

'So would I be right in saying that although you don't feel safe going to that part of town, you might be willing to go to somewhere nearer home?'

'When you said you had managed to handle that difficult conversation I could see you were relieved you had done it. How did you do it?'

'So despite the fact that you were beginning to panic, you found a way to keep going without giving in to it. That was brave.'

Coaches often use the metaphor of an iceberg to describe how much lurks below the surface. In this case what is below the surface and un-stated are not deeper problems, but possible solutions. A skilled coach will be intuitive about these opportunities. She will sense the nuances, the hints, the implications of what is being said or unsaid. On occasions she may make a speculative observation and test out the coachee's reaction.

Coach: Can I check that I heard you correctly? Would I be right in saying that at times you have to work hard to keep your spirits up in your present situation?

Coachee: Sometimes it is very hard to keep going.

Coach: It sounds tough for you. What have you found helpful in keeping your spirits up when things are not going well?

Coachee: I don't know, you have to keep going, there are no other choices.

Coach: It takes courage to keep going and I'm wondering what you say to yourself to allow you to do that.

Coachee: I tell myself that I have been through a lot and that I'm further forward than I was a few years ago.

Coach: When you look back at this time, what will you be most proud of in your ability to get through a tough time?

Coaching is an opportunity for coachees to 'get solutions off their chest' and test them out in a public space. The coach may encourage the coachee to rehearse in the meeting the actions he wants to perform. It is worth recalling that the solution focused way is to find small steps forward, micro-solutions, which accumulatively add up to major progress. Searching for a definitive, permanent solution is an illusion.

Be immediate. The solution focused coach works 'in the moment' and attends carefully to the dynamics of the session. By observing the coachee he/she will be able to pick up and reflect back shifts in their emotional and physical states.

Coach: I noticed that when you said you would like to travel, your whole face lit up and you became quite animated. It sounds like something you really want to do.

Coachee: You're right, it's a big thing for me. I'm desperate to break out and do something adventurous. I'm bored stiff with my routine, I feel like I'm a spectator watching everyone else have a good time.

Similarly the coach will pick up feelings that may not have been expressed openly but are nonetheless in the room.

Coach: I'm not sure if this is a helpful observation, but when I asked you about your relationship with your brother, you seemed to tense up.

Coachee: He drives me mad. He keeps saying he's going to do things then he fails to deliver. He and I argue a lot.

It is important for the coach to take stock during sessions to check out whether what she is doing is actually helpful. Failure to evaluate during the session can lead to the discovery at the end that you were trying to solve the wrong problem and that you have moved off the coachee's agenda. The coach may use questions such as:

• How are we getting on with this?
• Is this what you came to talk about today?
• Are we on the right track here?
• Is this helpful in generating new ideas?

Commonly made mistakes

Rushing into solutions. Coaches can take the title of the approach too literally and think that it bars coachees from talking about their concerns or difficulties. They become hypersensitive to any issue that does not immediately appear to be part of the solution. The premature seizing on apparent solutions can lead to superficial action plans, which fail to understand the process required to generate sustainable solutions.

Being too positive. While it is helpful to adopt a life-affirming approach and to bring a spirit of optimism into a coaching relationship, it is equally unhelpful to be positive about everything all of the time. An overly upbeat, 'always look on the bright side of life' attitude from the coach will lead some coachees to conclude that she doesn't really grasp the reality of their situation.

Problem-solving in disguise. The coach appears to consult with the coachee but she is convinced that she knows best and pushes solutions onto the coachee. Deep down the coach does not believe that the coachee is capable of finding solutions.

Over-complimenting. Giving regular positive feedback is an integral part of helping the coachee move from a problem mindset to a solution mindset. It provides a platform for launching new and challenging initiatives.However, it has to be tailored to the needs of the individual. Some people need more positive feedback than others.

Panicking when coachees don't follow the script. Solution focused coaching is deceptively simple, but not easy in practice. Novice coaches sometimes report that they initially make headway with their coachees, but at some point their solution-language dries up. They find it difficult to keep the focus and flow of the conversation. At times they can feel lost in the conversation and are unsure how to contribute. Another item the novice solution focused coach needs to come to terms with is that he/she is often working with a small amount of information. At times it may not even be clear what the coachee is talking about as he/she is unable to articulate concerns clearly. You need a certain amount of faith to do this. In some meetings the coach (and perhaps the coachee too) feel that it is going nowhere, that the conversation has become circular. It takes tenacity from the coach to hold on and keep working for the pivotal moment when the coachee discovers something of value. Most of the time the breakthrough comes, but not always.

When we are learning a new skill we usually feel awkward and incompetent to begin with. We need to accept that we do not have the same degree of control or authority. We may also find it difficult to go back to doing what we used to do. So for a while we feel trapped in a state of incompetence. We have lost what was familiar without enjoying the benefit of the new skill.

Be flexible. When the coaching conversation is not helping the coachee to move forward, there is little point in continuing with the same type of interventions. As Einstein said, 'Insanity is doing the same thing over and over again, expecting different results.' When coachees keep repeating failed solutions it is the coach who needs to take the initiative and 'do something different.' This could be to alter the pace or focus of the meeting. It could mean asking fewer questions and listening more, or acknowledging more explicitly the coachee's ambivalence. It could mean giving quite a different kind of assignment or no assignment at all.

The following are some tips to help in becoming fluent in this new language.

Practice tips for becoming fluent in solution language

- Go slowly at the beginning.
- Stay close to your coachee's agenda.
- Listen carefully to your coachee without rehearsing your response.
- Allow time to think about what your coachee has said.

Brief silences can be important.

- Make each of your responses connect with what the coachee has just said.
- Match your coachee's language sometimes, but at others convert problem statements into goals (reframe multi-problems multi-goals).
- Be as specific, clear and concrete in your language as possible e.g. What will you be doing that will tell you that you are more confident?
- Acknowledge your coachee's concerns and difficulties.
- Don't be too optimistic or try to persuade the coachee that he/she is making progress.
- Use humour to lighten the atmosphere.
- Be patient, trust the process and an opening will come!

Therapy research suggests that as much as 87 per cent of change is due, not to the therapeutic relationship or therapy model used, but to factors relating directly to the client; for example, their resources/networks/motivation and theory of change. The probability of success is associated with the therapist's willingness to match the client's views about the problem, possible solutions and the change process (Duncan and Miller, 1999). This finding fits well with the values and practices of solution focused coaching. We work with 'what's there'; we focus on coachee competence and resources; we keep them centre stage and ensure they take credit for any success; we facilitate their self-learning; we stay close to their agenda, goals and strategies. Over the past decade coaching research has dramatically increased so the many factors involved in coachee change and the coach–coachee relationship will be found (e.g. O'Broin and Palmer, 2010).

The skilled coachee

If the coachee is the crucial determining factor in a successful outcome, what might be the skills and qualities of the skilled coachee?

- Motivation – how much does the coachee want to achieve the goal and how willing is he/she to do what it takes?
- Open to learning – how able is the coachee to learn from experience? How flexible is he/she in his outlook? How capable is he/she of taking onboard feedback?
- Self-reliance – how independent is the coachee? How willing is he/she to view coaching as ultimately a DIY activity?
- Honesty and ability to trust – how much does the coachee believe in the coaching process? How much does the coachee respect and trust the coach? How realistic is the coachee in facing up to the reality of his or her situation?
- Has a viable theory of change – does the coachee have a realistic view as to how change takes place? Does the coachee have an internal locus of control and see him or herself as being a change agent? Does the coachee have a

realistic time framework for what he or she wants to achieve? Will the coach be able to match this theory of change?

- Listens as well as talks – how capable is the coachee of participating in a balanced and focused conversation? Does the coachee listen to the coach? Does the coachee listen to her or himself? Does the coachee listen to anyone?
- Uses his/her imagination – can the coachee envisage a preferred future? Can the coachee rehearse in his or her own mind the action that needs to taken? Can the coachee imagine taking initiatives rather than passively reacting to events?
- Walks the talk – can the coachee make decisions? Can the coachee do what's needed? Can the coachee adapt action plans? Can the coachee follow through?
- Resilience – how able is the coachee to stick at the task? Can the coachee come back from apparent failures or disappointments?

Coaches are responsible *to* but not *for* coachees. This may be self-evident, but it is an important ethical and professional principle. It emphasises the coach's duty to offer coachees a fair and ethical service, without crossing the boundary of a professional relationship. It warns against encouraging dependency or emotional involvement. Chapter Seven will explore these issues further.

Practice tips

- Observe how and when you use silence in your coaching approach.
- Observe your listening style and consider what helps or hinders your efforts to actively listen to your coachee. What distracts you; what is your internal dialogue during times when you are distracted from actively listening to your coachee; what might be a useful word or phrase to bring to mind at these times, in order to restore your trust in active listening?
- Practice curiosity and non-judgemental observation of your own and others' strengths and solutions.

- Pay attention to the overall flow of the coaching session, noting progress made towards the coachee's goals and steering discussion as appropriate within the given time constraints. Enquire how the coachee believes the session is progressing.
- Use imagery techniques to help the coachee fully visualise him/herself achieving their goal(s).
- Help the coachee learn to reflect on the language they use and the story they tell; what is helpful and what unhelpful; where might they alter the language they use to free themselves of any un-truths that have become established in their minds; how does this shift in language help them take the next steps towards their goals?
- Notice and reflect back any constructive thinking the coachee reveals in telling their story.

Discussion points

- To what extent do you believe there is a role for directive input in solution focused coaching? When is it appropriate to offer your own advice and solutions to the coachee's problem?
- When coaching, what role do your own emotions play in solution focused coaching? How should they be managed, utilised and/or expressed?
- In what contexts is it useful to interrupt your coachees during the coaching discussion?

Suggested reading

Berg, I.K. and Szabó, P. (2005) *Brief Coaching for Lasting Solutions*. New York: Norton.

Jackson, P.Z. and McKergow, M. (2006) *The Solutions Focus: Making Coaching and Change SIMPLE* (2nd edition). London: Nicholas Brealey Publishing.

Lazarus, A.A. (1984) *In the Mind's Eye*. New York: Guilford Press.

Palmer, S. and Whybrow, A. (Eds) (2007) *Handbook of Coaching Psychology: A Guide for Practitioners*. London: Routledge.

6

Group and team coaching

Solution focused coaching and the approach in general lends itself perfectly to group work and team development (McKergow and Clarke, 2005, 2007; Jackson and McKergow, 2007). The models and questions are simple yet effective, the emphasis is on positivity, inclusivity and empowerment, and the intention is to identify achievable, actionable step change. Whether you are bringing together a group of strangers or an established team, each individual should find solution focused coaching groups provide a supportive environment where it is easy to open up, talk freely about aspirations, recognise one's own strengths and achievements as well as those of others, and realise one's own and the team's potential.

The solution focused approach is effective in group and team coaching for a number of reasons (see Bill O'Connell, 2005), as follows:

- In general, individuals are more willing to talk about their strengths in a group setting than they are about their weaknesses. The solution focused approach quickly establishes an air of openness, trust and empowerment.
- The focus on solutions (not problems) and simple steps, and on utilisation of all the resources within the group, naturally builds energy levels and commitment to action.
- Individuals within the group quickly develop solution focused skills that others can find extremely supportive. This may encourage the development of a wider solution focused climate and culture.

In his excellent book *Solution Focused Groupwork*, John Sharry (2007) describes how the solution focused approach is a 'group-centred' as opposed to 'facilitator centred' interaction (Sharry, 2007), emphasising the potential power of the group dynamic for peer coaching and learning; discussion develops amongst the group, with group members speaking directly to each other as opposed to speaking via the coach or facilitator. Sharry also warns of the potential for negative modelling within the group and the importance of encouraging group support (see Sharry, 2007).

Solution focused coaching approaches have been successfully adapted for use with groups across different contexts including business, education, social work and the health sector (O'Connell, 2005), providing a brief but effective group intervention for coaching (Hoskisson, 2003; Grant, 2003; Green *et al.*, 2006; Spence and Grant, 2007; Green, Grant and Rynsaardt, 2007; Grant, 2008; Spence, Cavanagh and Grant, 2008; Yu, Collins, Cavanagh, White and Fairbrother, 2008; Grant, Curtayne and Burton, 2009). In this chapter we present solution focused coaching processes, models and activities for use in both group and team coaching.

Solution focused coaching models

The Reflecting Team model

A widely recognised process model for group solution focused coaching is the 'Reflecting Team model,' put forward by Harry Norman (Norman, 2003). Norman specifies a number of roles to be allocated within the group, namely that of presenter, process manager, time keeper and team member (Norman, 2003). Within the course of an SFC programme, each group member is given the opportunity to play each role. The presenter takes their turn to be the focus of attention and prepares to talk through the perceived problem, while the group listens to identify any resources and potential solutions the presenter might move forward with. It is the role of the process manager to direct discussion through the recommended phases, and of the time keeper to ensure conversation is progressing in a timely manner. Team member is an equally important role for listening to the presenter, listening for resources and questioning for exceptions, past successes and preferred future images.

Norman (2003) also describes the six steps of the Reflecting Team model process as follows:

1 preparing
2 presenting
3 clarifying
4 affirming
5 reflecting
6 concluding.

In the Preparing and Presenting stages the presenter outlines the current issue and what has been done so far. The group then asks SF questions to Clarify their understanding of the situation, with everyone having the opportunity to speak. The Affirming stage is for each member to offer a compliment to the presenter on their presentation. During the Reflecting stage, each member of the group builds on what has been said so far by offering their own ideas or views on the issue at hand. The presenter then Concludes the session by thanking the group for their contributions, and summarising what small steps they intend to take next as a result. See Norman (2003) for more details of this Reflecting Team model. The reflecting team model has also been effectively applied in solution focused supervision (O'Connell, 2005; Sharry, 2007), as detailed in Chapter Seven.

Alternative solution focused coaching group models

This section presents four further solution focused coaching models that may be effectively used for group or team coaching, with five, four and three steps respectively. The choice of model may depend on the purpose of the coaching, the make-up of the group and its familiarity with the overall solution focused coaching process. For consistency, we will continue to refer to the group member who is the present focus of attention as the 'presenter,' as in Norman's (2003) Reflecting Team model.

The OSKAR model

The OSKAR model, developed by Paul Jackson and Mark McKergow (2007) is well known and frequently used by those practicing solution focused coaching. The acronym OSKAR represents five key solution focused coaching steps as follows:

O   Outcome
S   Scaling
K   Know-how and resources
A   Affirm and action
R   Review

In the first step, Outcome, the coach and coachee establish what the coachee's objectives are for coaching, exploring their immediate goals for the coaching session, as well as their longer-term goals and desired future state. The next step is to utilise the Scaling technique to understand where, on a scale of one to ten, the coachee is today in terms of achieving their desired future state. In the step Know-how and resources the coach helps the coachee to identify what they are already doing well, their existing knowledge, skills and resources and exceptions where they are having success with the current challenge. Affirm and action is about identification of small actionable next steps. The final step of Review may take place at a later stage, to reflect on what is better since the last coaching session, what the coachee did to make things better and what they would like to do next. For more information on the OSKAR model see Jackson and McKergow's (2007) *The Solutions Focus: Making Coaching and Change SIMPLE.*

The FOCUS model

In Chapter Two we presented an eight-step model for solution focused coaching, with the acronym 'SOLUTION'. When working with groups or teams a more concise model may be appreciated, and for this purpose we offer a five-step solution focused coaching model with the acronym

'FOCUS,' as follows (also see Williams, Palmer and O'Connell, 2011):

F   Free talk
O   Openly explore goals
C   Consider exceptions and resources
U   Understand preferred future
S   Sign up to small steps

In the first step, the presenter is invited to Freely talk about themselves, their hobbies, any pre-session change and their presenting problem or challenge, including a scaling of one (low) to ten (high) of how confident they feel in dealing with this problem or challenge. In the second step the group Openly explore the presenter's goals, probing for past successes and current hopes and aspirations. The third step is to Consider exceptions; where has the problem been overcome, or not presented itself as much. The team members listen carefully for successes, resources and strengths that may be reflected back to the presenter. In the fourth step the intention is to Understand the presenter's preferred future, using variations of the Miracle Question (de Shazer, 1988) to help build a picture in the presenter's mind's eye of what success looks like, and what they will do to achieve this. The final step is to explore potential solutions that utilise the individual's signature strengths and skills, and for the presenter to Sign up to small steps by creating a simple action plan. The scaling question may be used again to revisit the presenter's confidence levels in dealing with the presenting problem, and to gage whether further exploration is needed, should they rate their confidence as less than seven out of ten.

The Probing for Solutions model

Anthony Grant put forward the Probing for Solutions model in the special report on solution focused coaching with four steps as follows (Palmer *et al.*, 2007):

1   Listen for solutions.
2   Probe for solutions.

3 Talk about solutions.
4 Plan for solutions.

In the first step the presenter describes the current problem or challenge while the group Listen carefully for solutions within the story. Next, the group Probe for solutions, asking questions to reveal any exceptions; where has the presenter been successful with a similar problem, or with an element of the current problem. The third step is to Talk about solutions, developing a clear vision of success using the Miracle Question (de Shazer, 1988) and other imagery techniques. It is particularly important for the group to listen for and reflect back strengths and resources that may help the presenter to achieve this vision of success. The final step is for the presenter to Plan for solutions, committing to specific, time-framed actions and scaling their confidence in completing these actions.

The three step solution focused coaching model

In his book *Solution Focused Stress Counselling* Bill O'Connell presents a three-step process model (O'Connell, 2001; 2004), which may be effectively applied in group or team solution focused coaching settings:

1 Problem talk.
2 Future talk.
3 Strategy talk.

The first step of the model, Problem talk, is for the coach and team members to listen while the presenter talks through their perceived problem, acknowledging their concerns and validating their situation. At this stage, to clarify the situation and provide a clear focus for the session, it can be instrumental to ask the presenter to summarise their problem in one word, and to put that one word in a sentence (O'Connell, 2001). The group then ask questions to help the presenter specify exactly what their goal is in relation the presenting problem. The second step, Future talk, is about helping the presenter to look to the future, and to imagine what success looks like, for example using the Miracle

Question. In the final step of Strategy talk, the group ask questions to help the presenter identify workable solutions and small steps that will start them on the journey of implementing that solution. The group listen for and reflect back all resources that the presenter brings into the session, such that the presenter may utilise these in developing their own, unique action strategy.

Group solution focused coaching

This section focuses on the unique aspects of designing and delivering a group solution focused coaching session for a disparate group of individuals, for example in employee assistance programmes (EAPs), stress management courses or generic solution focused coaching workshops. Key considerations are discussed and an outline of a solution focused coaching programme offered. Since a number of solution focused coaching models have been presented for use with groups, the example programme is purposefully generic, such that any one of these models may be selected by the reader and utilised within the programme.

Key considerations

There are a great many benefits of being part of a solution focused coaching group as opposed to being individually coached, including:

* The opportunity for shared learning.
* Recognition of oneself in the situations of others.
* Instant 'normalisation' of one's problems.
* Increased levels of validation.
* Development of one's own solution focused coaching skills.

In bringing together a group that do not necessarily know each other, it is important to invest time upfront in developing a climate of trust and confidentiality. As part of the introduction process, group members may contribute to, and sign up to, a set of ground rules concerning how they will work together, how the session and any breaks will be managed, and the commitment to be made regarding confidentiality of information within the group.

The positive focus of solution focused coaching on strengths, solutions and individual empowerment is instrumental in helping group members engage in the process, sharing concerns and thinking creatively about solutions within a mutually respectful and supportive context. The facilitator may lead by example by role-modelling the principles and approaches of solution focused coaching.

Managing difficult groups

In solution focused coaching each individual is to be held in high regard, and their unique perspective valued. In practice, faced with a 'difficult group,' where one or more of the group members do not seem on board with the process, this takes great skill and patience on the part of the coach to deliver. From an inclusive solution focused perspective one might consider the following:

* Reframing your view of the 'difficult' or 'resistant' group (de Shazer, 1984); what might be a more helpful description?
* Trusting in the solution focused coaching approach, in your own skills as a coach and in the group's problem solving capabilities.
* Where in the cycle of change (Prochaska and DiClemente, 1986) is each group member? Connect with each individual where they are presently. See Chapter Eight for more information and example questions.
* Everything said has meaning; what story is the group member telling? Of the scripts they reveal, which are helpful and which unhelpful to them?
* As Sharry suggests, look for 'strengths in the client's position or for positive intentions and goals with which they can co-operate' (2007: 43).
* Allow each group member to stay with problem-talk for as long as they need; this will validate their concerns and help them, in their own time, to shift their focus from problem to solution.

Example group solution focused coaching programme

The following is intended as a guide for those developing a group solution focused coaching programme (see Table 6.1).

Positioning

In the pre-programme information, and at the start of the programme itself, it is useful to outline the solution focused coaching groups' purpose and aims, the solution focused coaching process and essential housekeeping. As a group they will have the opportunity to participate in group coaching, to make progress on personal goals as well as developing solution focused coaching skills. Each group member will be invited in turn to talk through their perceived goal for coaching, and to be coached by the group using a solution focused approach.

Table 6.1 **Example group coaching agenda**

Session	Content
Positioning	SFC groups' purpose and aims Housekeeping (toilets, fire escapes, timings etc) Introductions
Contracting	Ways of working – confidentiality, ground rules, role of facilitator
Goal clarification	Work in pairs/trios to clarify personal goals Review as a group to establish common group goals
What is SFC	SFC principles Warm up exercise – how it feels to focus on strengths versus weaknesses SFC process SFC skills based exercises
Group coaching	Presenter 1 Presenter 2 Presenter 3
Review	Appreciative feedback for the Presenters and other group members
Close	SF style group feedback on meeting Overview of subsequent meetings

Pre-programme information might also encourage participants to:

- Consider what they see as their coaching goal; what do they hope to change as a result of the coaching programme?
- Reflect on what they see as their personal strengths, skills and resources.
- Observe any change to their situation or progress made towards their goal, prior to the group's first meeting.

At the start of the first meeting, introductions might include names, expectations for the coaching group, and a positive outcome that they have achieved recently, whether at home or work, for example fixing the door on the garden shed, making it to the gym, winning a client pitch or completing expenses on time!

Within your meeting agenda it is highly recommended that time is given to 'problem-free talk.' During problem-free talk group members are encouraged to explore how they spend any leisure time they have, their interests, hobbies and preferences. This exercise can reveal strengths and resources that may be used to generate solutions to current challenges. It is also an excellent way for the group to get to know each other.

Contracting

It is particularly important to establish ways of working and confidentiality agreements at the outset of the programme. Ground rules may be generated by the group on flip charts, covering what is expected of group members, the group as a whole and the facilitator. These flip charts may be kept to be revisited in future meetings and reviewed at the close of the solution focused coaching programme.

Goal clarification

Group members may be invited to work in pairs or trios to discuss and clarify their personal coaching goals: what do they see as their goal(s); what would they like to achieve as a result of the coaching; what progress have they already made; what strengths, skills and resources do they have that might be useful to them?

Coming back together as a whole group to review what has been discussed provides an ideal opportunity to establish common group goals. As the coach, highlight similarities across group member goals, gaining agreement to topics that might be useful for the group to address together (Sharry, 2007).

What is solution focused coaching?

The facilitator may take time upfront to verbally outline the principles and process of solution focused coaching. A comparison warm up exercise may be useful in order to demonstrate the effectiveness of a positive solution focused approach. Group members may be asked to work in pairs or trios, to talk about a development need, feeding back as a group on the experience. The process is then repeated with the new instruction to talk about a personal strength. Typically, while some may initially find it less comfortable talking about personal strengths, the level of energy in the room does increase, and the group tend to feedback how much more empowering it is to talk about strengths as opposed to weaknesses. This demonstrates the principles of solution focused coaching, which focuses on identification of strengths and resources, what has worked well in the past, what a preferred future looks like and small steps to achieve it.

The facilitator may then select and share a solution focused coaching model and list of questions, such that the group is aware of the fundamental principles, process and techniques of solution focused coaching. Attention may be drawn to solution focused coaching concepts and techniques such as problem talk, scaling, curiosity, the Miracle Question (de Shazer, 1988) and small steps. In later sessions, the group may benefit from skills-based exercises aimed at revisiting these solution focused coaching techniques (Sharry, 2007). Invite the group to work in pairs or trios to practice a specific technique, working on an aspect of their coaching goal and at the same time developing their solution focused coaching skills as well as their connection to others within the group.

Group coaching

As each group member is invited to take the role of 'presenter,' a useful start point is to invite them to talk through their pre-programme reflections: how might they describe their goals for coaching; what do they see as their personal strengths; what, if any, pre-session change did they observe; what did they do and what resources did they use to result in this change? As facilitator, guide the presenter and group members through the steps of your chosen solution focused coaching model, and as a group explore the presenter's goal whilst listening for signature solutions, strengths, skills resources and untapped potential. Each coaching discussion closes with the presenter thanking the group and summarising the next steps they intend to take in order to make progress on their goals; the strengths they are likely to use and what they are going to do more of to achieve the desired results.

Twenty minutes is suggested per presenter. The number of group members to present during the first meeting will depend upon the time available for the session. Those who do not present at this first meeting may be encouraged to prepare to do so in the next meeting.

Review and close

Appreciative feedback is invited from the group on the contributions made by each participant, whether in the role of presenter, process manager, time keeper or team member. As coach it is useful to encourage development of a group identity by highlighting the strengths of the group, and the ways in which the group has worked well together (Sharry, 2007).

To close the meeting, solution focused feedback may be invited on how the programme has been presented and how the first meeting has been experienced. The final comments may be to provide an overview of how subsequent meetings might run.

Team solution focused coaching

Katzenbach and Smith (1993: 45) describe a team as:

> a small number of people with complementary skills who are committed to a common purpose, performance goals, and approach for which they hold themselves mutually accountable.

In his instrumental book *Coaching the Team at Work*, Clutterbuck (2007) describes the central role of communication, mutual support and adaptive working styles in effective team working. Team members need to be skilled at goal setting, planning, conflict resolution and collaborative problem solving (Clutterbuck, 2007). In this way there is significant alignment between the characteristics of effective teams and the process and skills of solution focused coaching.

Teams are typically built with a purpose in mind, and that purpose is often linked to a change agenda such as targeted product development, service improvement or increased organisational efficiency. The ethos of solution focused coaching is one of creative, pragmatic simplicity, and the aim is for achievable progressive change, making solution focused coaching ideal for team development.

Clutterbuck (2007: 77) describes team coaching as 'helping the team improve performance, and the processes by which performance is achieved, through reflection and dialogue.' A solution focused coaching programme brings team members together and encourages them to recognise their own strengths and achievements, and the strengths and achievements of others. It fosters appreciation for the capability and resources within the team and focuses team efforts on simple, shared, agreed goals. In this way, solution focused coaching has been described as 'an antidote to a blame culture' (O'Connell, 2005: 134). Through the solution focused coaching process the team works together to consider what has worked well in the past and how to do more of this, what to stop doing, and what they might try that is different.

In this section we discuss solution focused coaching team dynamics and present an example team solution focused coaching agenda with a range of solution focused coaching team exercises, before considering the role of the team leader in solution focused coaching, use of 360 degree feedback and the creation of a solution focused climate and culture.

Solution focused coaching team dynamics

From a solution focused coaching perspective, based on the insights of Milton Erickson and Steve de Shazer, the team may be viewed as a skilled problem solving force that has the resources it needs to find solutions that will work for them. In team solution focused coaching programmes, participants come together to work through real, live business challenges. The focus is on progression of individual, team and organisational goals. An additional benefit is the acquisition of solution focused coaching skills among team members, use of which could facilitate a transition to a solution focused coaching climate and culture within the team and wider organisation.

As coach, it is important to understand the team dynamics as much as possible. Box 6.1 lists questions for consideration in advance of the first meeting.

Box 6.1 Preparatory questions for team coaching

- What is the purpose and objective of the team?
- Why is the team participating in solution focused coaching? Is it voluntary?
- How is the team performing?
- To what extent are they working effectively as a team?
- What are their strengths as a team?
- What is it that they want to achieve? What are their team goals?
- What types of challenges does the team face?
- Who is the team manager and what role do they play?
- Who are the team members and what are their roles?
- What is the current team culture and climate?

The team manager and team members are in the best position to answer these questions. Prior to launching the solution focused coaching programme, speak with the team manager to understand their expectations of team coaching and their views on the questions above. Where possible also speak with team members, being transparent about how the information gathered will be used and shared. Senior sponsorship of the solution focused coaching programme and involvement of the team manager as a solution focused coaching role model are two significant factors that can directly influence the success of the coaching intervention.

An example team solution focused coaching programme

The following is intended as a guide for those developing a team solution focused coaching programme (Table 6.2). A range of solution focused coaching exercises are suggested that may be utilised as appropriate to the team's needs at different stages of the programme.

Positioning and contracting

As in group coaching, it is important to contract ground rules and ways of working with the team at the start of the first meeting, and to gather expectations of the coaching process. A warm up exercise may be useful to focus the group's attention, exploring team purpose; team objectives; successes to date; current challenges; team strengths; what they have done well and how these successes/strengths may be utilised in the future. Ideally the team will agree to the solution focused coaching principles of full group participation, mutual respect, listening to all, focusing on strengths, giving of praise and problem-free solution talk.

As a team they will have the opportunity to focus on team performance goals, at the same time identifying personal strengths goals and developing solution focused coaching skills.

Table 6.2 **Example team coaching agenda**

Session	Content
Positioning	SFC groups' purpose and aims Housekeeping (toilets, fire escapes, timings etc) Introductions and problem-free talk
Contracting	Ways of working – confidentiality, ground rules, role of facilitator
Goal clarification	Clarification of team performance goal(s) Discussion of pre-session change
What is SFC	SFC principles Warm up exercise – how it feels to focus on strengths versus weaknesses SFC process SFC skills based exercises
Identification of team strengths	Identification of team strengths
Identification of personal strengths	Identification of team member strengths Review of pre-course questionnaires Pair/trio discussions and group review
Team coaching	Team coaching
Review	Individual reflection time Consolidation of action plans Discuss and agree support processes
Close	SF style group feedback on meeting Overview of subsequent meetings

Goal clarification

As part of the first meeting, the team will need time to clarify and reach agreement on what they see as their team performance goal(s). Possible activities include:

- *Problem talk* It is important to acknowledge the difficulties faced by the team before moving onto solution generation. The solution focused approach leads to the validation of the team's concerns without over-analysis or attribution of blame.
- *Problem focused versus solution focused scripts* See Chapter Nine for details of this exercise.
- *Small steps* This exercise is described in Chapter Nine and has been adapted here for use with teams.

Prepare two flips with the titles 'Problem' and 'Small steps' respectively. Ask each team member to write what they see as the team's current problem or challenge, and to write on the Small steps flip one small step that could be taken to make progress against that particular problem. Then ask a volunteer to tear up the Problem flip, and to talk through the Small steps flip. As a group, explore the benefits of each action and who will take responsibility, scale team confidence levels and clarify how the team will know when these steps have been taken.

- *Four boxes* If further goal clarification is needed, an adaptation of the four boxes exercise described in Chapter Nine may be useful. Prepare four flips for each of the four segments: issue, preferred outcome, resources and scaling position. Post these up around the room and ask the team to add their observations of each, before coming together to discuss the content of the flips, and to generate next steps.

- *Scaling walk exercise* This exercise is described in Chapter Nine and has been adapted here for use with teams. Focus the team by asking them to describe the current problem or challenge. Place ten pieces of paper with the numbers one to ten written on them on the floor, and invite each team member to stand on the number they think best describes the team's current situation with the given problem. For example, where 1 is not in control and 10 is fully in control. Ask the team members on different numbers to describe their perspectives. Then ask team members to turn to face the number ten, and say what they see there; what small steps might be taken to move a step closer to ten?

What is solution focused coaching?

The following are adaptations of exercises that may be useful when introducing teams to the principles and first stages of solution focused coaching.

- *Problem free talk* This is about getting to know the 'team' as a whole. Explore with the team – what is the team's identity; what is the team's interests, beliefs, passions, attitudes, drivers, humour and values; how does the team think, feel and act? (Hutchins, 1989)

- *Pre-session change* Participants may be set a task in advance of the first group meeting, to notice any change in the team performance, team results and/or the impact of team on other teams/client groups. Participants are then invited to share these insights in the first team meeting, exploring how that positive change happened, and what they did as a team to achieve it.

- *Profiling a solution focused coaching team* – this exercise is aimed at understanding what 'good' looks like for a solution focused team. Imagine the team has been transformed overnight in to a solution focused team; coming in to work the next day, what do they notice that is different? What values do they now hold; what qualities are they displaying; how are they communicating and working together; how are they supporting and challenging each other; what does it feel like to be part of the team; what do others in the organisation see?

- *Solution focused team narrative* Some teams may find it useful to tell the story of the team so far, before moving on to build the vision of its preferred future. This may be done creatively with story boards or other ideas adapted from narrative coaching. The aim is to identify transferable skills and signature solutions from what the team have already achieved.

Identification of team strengths

Encourage the team to identify the strengths of the team as a whole, through exercises such as the following:

- *Team profile* Encourage the team to work together to build a team profile; what are the strengths, resources and capabilities of the team? What are the team's core competencies, abilities, skills, experiences, achievements and signature solutions?

- *Team types* A team type instrument such as Belbin team types (Belbin, 1981; 1993) may be adopted to understand the different personalities and preferred ways of working within the team, to acknowledge similarities and differences among team members, and to recognise the strengths that each team type has to offer. The team may explore how they maximise on the strengths of each team type currently, and how to do so more in the future.

- *'How did we do that' exercise* The purpose here is to review past successes in order to identify team strengths and forgotten solutions; at the time that we achieved this past success, how were we thinking and feeling, what were we doing, what was the context; what works for us as a team; what skills can we transfer to help with the current problem/challenge; when are we at our best as a team; are there any inherited scripts that are part of the problem?

- *Identifying exceptions* Split the team into sub-groups and ask the groups to reflect on examples of solutions already in use by the team; what results have the team achieved and what were the success behaviours; what have been significant wins; what challenges have the team successfully overcome and how did the team achieve this? Come back together to review as a whole team.

- *Living with change* This exercise is described in Chapter Nine and has been adapted here for use with teams. Ask the team to generate examples where the team has lived with change. Listing these on a flip, invite each team member to allocate three ticks for the three examples that best represent a time when the team coped well and got the best out of the change. Break out into sub-groups to explore the top three examples, identifying strengths, resources and skills that resulted in the team thriving through that change. Re-group to share insights as a whole team.

Identification of personal strengths

A variety of approaches may be used to help team members identify their personal strengths. Hoskisson (2003) describes how participants can work in pairs to share and explore what they are good at. An exercise may be centred on the creation of individual strengths profiles, listing personal qualities and traits, values and attitudes, interests, drivers, positive impacts, abilities, skills and personal or work achievements. The 'Bringing out the best' exercise for exploring past successes is described in Chapter Nine. Facilitators may also like to consider pre-programme questionnaires, or psychometric strength finder tools such as the Centre of Applied Positive Psychology (CAPP)'s Realise2 tool.

Team coaching

A unique goal of team coaching is to transfer the skills of solution focused coaching to all group members. As coach, select and share a solution focused group coaching model. An activity may be facilitated whereby group members generate a set of SFC questions. Consideration should be given to any pairings/small group compositions during the team coaching, acknowledging any potential sensitivities and team dynamics.

The following solution focused coaching activities may prove useful during team coaching, to help the team further clarify their team performance goal(s), to recognise team strengths and signature solutions, and to agree actionable steps to achieve these goals.

- *Preferred future imagery, or 'The Miracle Question'* Facilitate the team to imagine their future desired state. An adaptation of de Shazer's (1988) Miracle Question may be used here: Imagine the team goes home tonight, each team member has a phenomenally good sleep, and the team is transformed overnight. Imagine this has happened and it's the next day – on coming back into the office, what's the first thing that they notice; what impact is the team having; what results are they achieving and how are they behaving in order to do this; how does it feel to be part of the team; how is the dynamic between individuals; what does the team climate feel like; what do they notice that's different; what are they doing differently?

- *Notice, Pretend and Do Something Different assignments* To maintain the focus on team as opposed to individual goals, it will be important for the team to agree the focus of these assignments and how the team will feedback and review their observations. Box 6.2 describes these homework assignments in more detail.

Box 6.2 Homework assignments

Notice assignments – notice assignments are where team members observe (in a non-judgemental, SF way!) any progress made with the team goals, and opportunities seen/taken to utilise their SFC skills. Team members may be invited to share these insights at the start of the next group meeting.

Pretend assignments – team members are encouraged to identify areas in which the team might 'act as if' they have achieved their goal; that the changes they desire have already happened. These insights may be shared at the beginning of the next meeting. See Chapter Four for more details.

Do something different assignments – team members are encouraged to identify something that the team might try doing differently, changing the frequency or rate of doing something, the timing or duration of it, the location etc. See Chapter Four for more details.

- *Being curious* Working in two groups, one group is asked to write down curiosity behaviours on post it notes, while the other group writes down behaviours indicating the opposite. These depictions may be shared as a whole group, and the benefits of being curious in solution focused coaching explored.
- *Goal stoppers* See Chapter Nine for more details on this exercise.
- *Signature solutions* An exercise of enquiry to identify the team's signature solution pattern; unique ways of

handling difficulties that have worked for them as a team over a long period of time. See Chapter Three for more details.

Review and close

Team members may appreciate individual reflection time, as well as time as a team, to summarise the next steps they intend to take in order to make progress on their team performance goal(s), the strengths they are likely to use and what they are going to do more of to achieve the desired results.

Invite appreciative feedback on the team's contributions during the meeting, on the progress made on their team performance goal(s) and on the coaching process overall – what has worked well and what might be done differently next time? Explore with the team the extent to which the team's coaching goals have been met, and whether or not a further team coaching meeting will be of benefit.

The role of the team manager

As with most talent development interventions in the workplace, the success of the solution focused coaching programme may be significantly influenced by the team manager. The team manager is naturally positioned to role model the solution focused principles both during and in-between solution focused coaching meetings, and as such it is important to ensure they are comfortable with and bought into the principles and practices of solution focused coaching, and to provide them with support as needed.

Solution focused and 360 degree feedback

360 degree feedback tools are commonplace within many organisations and, if implemented well, can act as an effective vehicle for the provision of feedback. From a solution focused perspective, the tone and content of the 360 degree feedback discussion may be quite different. The questionnaire output is explored to identify both strengths and development areas as usual; however the focus then shifts to

visualisation of the desired future state, formation of development goals and identification of strengths, resources, and signature solutions that can help the individual to achieve these changes.

Developing a team solution focused climate and culture

Team climates and organisational cultures develop and evolve over long periods of time. This may be understood from a gestalt perspective, appreciating that the whole is greater than the sum of the parts. When teams choose to adopt a solution focused approach to their work, this changes their whole way of working, their language, behaviour and underlying values. It becomes written into the narrative of the team. Other teams or departments observe the impact and results achieved, and experience a positive difference in their interactions with the solution focused team. If the solution focused approach has senior sponsorship and is role modelled consistently, overtime a ripple effect may be observed throughout the organisation and a solution focused organisational culture achieved.

Practice tips

- Invest time upfront contracting ways of working and confidentiality agreements with the group.
- Acknowledge problems and challenges before moving onto solutions.
- Focus on strengths, desired future states, solutions and small steps.
- Share solution focused skills to enable peer coaching, feedback and supervision.
- Select a solution focused process model to maintain the advantages of a disciplined approach to coaching.
- Maximise on the benefits of the group dynamic, and be sensitive to any team politics.
- Encourage senior sponsorship of solution focused coaching within the organisation, and support the team manager as a key role model.

- Utilise a range of tools as appropriate to help the group or team identify strengths and understand their potential.
- Don't push too hard too quickly for change as this can be de-motivating.

Discussion points

- To what extent is your group or team coaching 'Group-centred' as opposed to 'Facilitator-centred' (see Sharry, 2007)?
- Which of the group and team solution focused coaching models are likely to work best within your own coaching practice?
- How do the solution focused coaching models presented integrate with your existing approach to group and team coaching?
- What are effective ways of solution focused coaching with challenging groups?
- What approaches might you take to help an organisation develop a solution focused coaching climate and culture?

Suggested reading

Clutterbuck, D. (2007) *Coaching the Team at Work*. London: Nicholas Brealey International.

McKergow, M. and Clarke, J. (2005) *Positive Approaches to Change: Applications of Solutions Focus and Appreciative Inquiry at Work*. Cheltenham: SolutionsBooks.

Sharry, J. (2007) *Solution Focused Groupwork* (2nd edition). London: Sage Publications.

7

Professional, ethical and practice issues

This chapter considers the process of solution focused coaching, the coach–coachee relationship, the role of technology, ethical issues and supervision.

The coaching process

Solution focused coaching, like any other form of coaching, works best when neither coach nor coachee are distracted by logistical or process issues. The best way to ensure that a session runs smoothly is to plan for it. Take the time upfront to arrange and communicate session details – where will you meet, and at what time? Is the meeting space a neutral, comfortable and confidential one? Will you have access to all the materials you need, from water and tissues to technology? Who will be in attendance? What can they expect from the coaching engagement; is there a briefing document or agenda to be communicated?

Solution focused approaches are widely referred to as 'brief.' This means that it adopts the aim of achieving goal-focused change for the client as quickly and as simply as possible, focusing on the present and future and avoiding over-analysis of the past (O'Connell, 2005). In solution focused coaching, it is normal practice to encourage independence in the coachee, with a shared aim of them becoming their own coach. Given this, the tendency is to view each session as complete in itself, and to end each session by reviewing the extent to which the coachee's goal has been achieved, and whether or not any further sessions will be helpful (O'Connell, 1998, 2005; Cavanagh and Grant, 2010). You might provide an indication of a typical number of sessions, so all parties can envisage the beginning, middle and end of the coaching process. The actual number of sessions may vary depending on the format and purpose of coaching, but may be a one-off session, or more typically a series of three to five sessions over several months.

In our experience, the frequency and duration of sessions will depend on the purpose of the solution focused coaching; whether individual or group coaching; and the number of solution focused facilitators present. Generally, work place coaching sessions take place every two to four weeks, as this avoids putting undue pressure on coachees alongside other work and life events, and allows time in between sessions for the coachee to make progress with their agreed actions. Each session may last anything from ten minutes (for an individual brief solution focused intervention) to three hours or a full day (for a group or team session), but is more typically forty-five minutes to one hour and thirty minutes long.

The contracting process is essential, as it helps to build levels of trust early on between coach and coachee, and/or between coaching group members. Individuals and groups will often be reassured by a discussion of what can be expected from the solution focused coaching process, as well as from that day's session, and by agreeing what a good outcome will look like. In group or team coaching, all participants may contribute to setting clear ground rules, such as how to manage timings, breaks and interruptions, ways of working together and confidentiality. If you, as coach and facilitator, intend to take notes, it is important to draw attention to this, explain how these notes will be used and stored and gain agreement from the coachee or coaching group.

The coach–coachee relationship

From a systems perspective, there are three notable elements within the coach–coachee relationship; the coach, the coachee and the interaction between the two.

For the coach, any given coaching engagement will represent an opportunity for them to develop their experience, skills and resources as a coach. It is an opportunity to engage in the art of active listening, reflecting back and reframing, and to act as process manager so that the session flows according to the discipline of solution focused coaching. An effective solution focused coach is curious, non-judgemental and non-directive (Grant, 2006a).

For the coachee, it is an opportunity to partake in self-directed learning with the support of the coach, to make progress against specified goals, to recognise their own capabilities and at the same time develop their own resources as a self-coach by internalising solution focused coaching skills (Neenan and Palmer, 2001). For coaching to work, Grant identified that the coachee needs 'to be discontent with the present . . . to have a vision of the future . . . [and] to have the skills to do the work of change' (Grant, 2006a: 79).

The coach–coachee relationship develops as a product of the dynamic interaction between these two elements. Key solution focused coaching principles impacting upon the coach–client relationship are summarised in Box 7.1.

Box 7.1   Solution focused coaching principles influencing the coach–coachee relationship

- The coachee is held in high regard, viewed as a competent individual capable of resolving their own issues
- The coach encourages self-directed learning (Grant, 2006a)
- The coach focuses on creating an empowered learning environment: respectful; positive and strengths-based; forward looking, goal focused and action-orientated
- The coach acknowledges and validates concerns and problems whilst encouraging the coachee to avoid over analysis
- The coachee is viewed as the expert and the coach 'keeps out of the client's way' (O'Connell and Palmer, 2007: 281)

The solution focused coach–client relationship has been described as 'respectful, egalitarian, [and] collaborative'

(O'Connell and Palmer, 2007: 282). The purpose of solution focused coaching is to facilitate the coachee's thinking such that they identify for themselves the most effective solutions for the future. The role of the coach is to help the coachee recognise their own strengths, competencies and resources; to explore their past successes in order to identify signature solutions; and to highlight untapped potential or forgotten solutions. (Also see Palmer and McDowall, 2010.)

There may be times when the coachee appears to be resistant of the coaching process. Greene and Grant (2003) provide a useful account of this, exploring the change cycle (Prochaska and DiClemente, 1986) and encouraging the coach to understand where in the change cycle the coachee is in order to understand what they might be ready to commit to. The coach is advised to roll with resistance and to emphasise the coachee's freedom of choice (Greene and Grant, 2003), and to avoid solution focused becoming 'solution forced' (O'Connell, 2005) by ensuring that the coachee is not rushed at each stage of the coaching process. This is explored further in Chapter Eight.

Use of technology

The practice of coaching has historically been more traditional, valuing the face-to-face interaction. Times change however, and technology provides some potentially powerful ways of delivering therapy and coaching that are in keeping with our coachee's busy lives (e.g. Palmer, 2004). Open-minded approaches to the use of technology in coaching align well to the principles of solution focused coaching:

- Take the most pragmatic, simple approach.
- Do what works best for the client.
- Do something different.

Coaches may find it useful to meet face-to-face for at least the first coaching session. Subsequent sessions may, however, be more effectively delivered via the telephone, if this is the most convenient and realistic way for the coachee to attend. With the evolution of mobile phone technology communication has become more informal, and this may be embraced through the use of text messaging as an agreed method of communication.

The Internet has great capability for more creative coaching delivery channels. Email provides an efficient way of sharing information and confirming plans, whilst webcam technology such as Skype means that coaching may be delivered across geographical distances without losing the benefits of the coach and coachee being able to see each other's facial expressions. Web conferencing technologies similarly allow coach and coachee to share and view live documents during an online coaching session.

Telephone and web-based coaching may benefit from greater attention to process structure, as well as additional questions aimed at checking the coachee's thoughts and feelings about the progress of the coaching session. It is important to contract upfront and to have a clear agreement on how to manage distractions and interruptions that may arise during the coaching session.

Contacting each other outside of the coaching session can also become an issue if not first discussed at the contracting stage. For example, Skype indicates when contacts are online and it is too easy for a coachee to note that their coach is online and then to send them a message or call them. Likewise the coach could be tempted to contact their coachee too.

Ethical issues

Attending to ethical issues is important for the protection of the coach, coachee and client organisation. Practitioners are advised to work within the ethical boundaries established for their relevant professional bodies. Examples for coaching practitioners include the Association for Coaching Code of Ethics and Good Coaching Practice; and for coaching psychologists is the British Psychological Society (BPS) Code of Ethics and Conduct. For solution focused practitioners including coaches there is the United Kingdom Association for Solution Focused Practice Code of Ethics (UKASFP) (2008).

The BPS Code of Ethics and Conduct identifies four domains of responsibility: respect, competence, responsibility and integrity (BPS, 2009: 9). While each of these applies to solution focused coaching, the domain of Respect is something that is intrinsic to the philosophy and principles of solution focused coaching. It highlights the fundamental value of respecting the worth, self-determination, knowledge and expertise of the coachee. Ethical codes typically address critical issues such as the protection of human rights, of the mental health and psychological well-being of coach and coachee, and of data protection.

As stated previously in Chapter Five, coaches are responsible to, and not for, coachees. In contrast to counselling practices offered to a clinical population for the purpose of addressing psychological disturbances, coaching is more often a service provided to a non-clinical population for the purpose of progressive change on personal or performance goals. In solution focused coaching, the coachee is responsible for him/herself, and as such a contract is agreed in which the coachee takes responsibility for him/herself within the coaching process. The coach remains responsible to the coachee, and as such focuses on the provision of a fair and ethical service, respecting confidentiality and encouraging independence, as discussed below. However, an overarching principle of the UKASFP Code of Ethics is (2008: 1): 'As a solution focused practitioner, you must protect the health and wellbeing of people who use or need your services in every circumstance.'

Fair and ethical service

- Solution focused practitioners are encouraged to work within the boundaries of their professional technical competence, knowledge and experience.
- In accordance to solution focused principles, most ethical codes adopt an advisory tone, and respect that the practitioner will need to make use of their professional skill and judgement when making decisions relating to ethical issues.
- Solution focused practitioners are encouraged to refer coaching clients on as appropriate. Some coachees may require greater levels of psychological support and may

benefit from a referral to their doctor, a psychologist or psychotherapist (AC, 2010).

- The BPS code states the need for 'reflective practice, peer support and transparency of professional activity' (BPS, 2009: 7). A solution focused coaching practitioner is encouraged to engage in solution focused coaching supervision and self-review of their coaching practices, seeking to understand what has worked well and what they might do differently to support their clients in future sessions. Solution focused coaching also incorporates review of the coaching experience as part of the coaching process.

Confidentiality

- Given that a number of stakeholders are likely to exist in work place coaching interventions, it is important to establish a clear contract of confidentiality upfront, and to agree how and when feedback will be provided to each party. The contract is less complicated within life or personal coaching as there are usually no third parties involved. The UKASFP Code of Ethics item 2 states (2008:2):

  2) Respect the confidentiality of your clients;
  You must only use information about a client:

  – to continue to care for that person; or
  – for purposes where that person has given you
    specific permission to use the information; or
  – to take necessary steps to minimise and prevent the
    risks of clients harming themselves or others.

- The solution focused practitioner is encouraged to maintain appropriate and transparent records of coaching meetings, in accordance with the 1998 Data Protection Act.

Encouragement of independence

- The Association for Coaching states the need for 'openness with regards to coaching methods, techniques and coaching process' (AC, 2010). Solution focused practices actively encourage the coach to be transparent with their methods, offering the coachee clear explanations of the coaching tools and techniques in use. Transparency with methods naturally leads to the transfer of coaching skills and knowledge from coach to coachee, which is an additional advantage.

- The Association for Coaching also state the need to respect the coachee's right to end the coaching engagement at any point (AC, 2010). Solution focused practices actively encourage this by reviewing the need for any further coaching at the end of each session.
- Solution focused practitioners are advised to avoid any and all emotional involvement with their coachee.

On the occasions that ethical dilemmas do arise, it is rare that the solution is clear cut; the coach is likely to need to give great consideration to the best way forward, and is advised to consult their supervisor. Three ethical dilemmas are provided for the reader's consideration in Boxes 7.2, 7.3 and 7.4.

Box 7.2 Ethical dilemma: Fair and ethical service

You are part way through a coaching intervention with an individual employee in an organisation. The commissioning client is the HR department, and the coaching contract was agreed during a meeting with the employee and their line manager. In the third session, in your professional opinion, it becomes apparent that the employee is showing signs of clinical depression. You facilitate a discussion with the coachee on this matter, suggesting that a referral to a qualified counsellor would be more appropriate as they are experienced to meet the coachee's needs in this area. The coachee states very clearly that they do not want to be referred, and that they wish for this conversation to remain confidential. What do you do?

Box 7.3 Ethical dilemma: Confidentiality

A client organisation instructs you to work with an underperforming team; your commissioning client is the team manager, and they state very clearly their expectation that you pass on any information regarding team morale and motivation. During the sessions the team express their dissatisfaction with the team manager and state their intentions to leave the organisation, but despite you having stated at the outset that you have a responsibility to pass information back to the team manager, they ask that you respect the confidentiality of the coaching arrangement and do not pass on this information. What do you do?

Box 7.4 Ethical dilemma: Encouragement of independence

You have been coaching an individual for six months now. At the close of each session you review progress against goals with the coachee and question whether there is need for any further coaching. Despite having made good progress, from the coachee's reactions it is your professional opinion that they are becoming increasingly dependent upon you, and may be becoming over-reliant on you as a source of attention and personal validation, possibly forming an emotional attachment. What do you do?

Supervision

Hawkins and Smith (2006: 147) define supervision as 'the process by which a coach/mentor/consultant with the help of a supervisor, who is not working directly with the client, can attend to understanding better both the client system and themselves as part of the client-coach/mentor system, and transform their work.' This definition reflects the multiple functions of supervision and also the transformational aspects. Currently supervision is highly valued within the practice of coaching (see Hawkins and Smith, 2006). While you may need to invest a little time upfront in order to find the right supervision arrangement for you, it can bring significant benefits in terms of personal learning and development as a coach, and provides an important source of support on ethical issues and concerns (McDougall, 2008). Coaching supervision may be taken as an individual or as part of a group, and may be conducted in person, by telephone, the Internet or email/postal supervision (AC, 2005).

The principles of solution focused coaching may also be applied to supervision, as follows (see O'Connell, 2005):

- The focus is on the supervisee/s, and what they are doing, as opposed to the details of their coachees.
- Clear, incremental learning goals are set and previous solutions explored.
- Positive reinforcement and feedback is offered, with a focus on the supervisee's strengths, what they have done well and what they can do more of.
- A collaborative, non-directive approach is taken such that the supervisor questions and listens for the supervisee to discover their own creative solutions (Thomas, 1994).
- Solution focused techniques are utilised such as scaling, exception seeking, competency and strength finding and the Miracle Question (de Shazer, 1988).

Bill O'Connell (2005) offers a simple, five-step model for SF supervision:

1 Negotiate session goals.
2 Work with the supervisee's strengths and solutions.
3 Focus on the future.
4 Scale progress.
5 End the supervision process.

Solution focused principles can similarly be applied to group or team supervision, which is typically set up in a non-hierarchical way, with specific roles being allocated to different members of the group for each supervisee's review slot. For example, Norman (2003) developed the reflecting team model in which the supervisee in question becomes the presenter, and other group members take on the roles of process manager, time keeper and team members. Norman (2003) recommends the steps of preparation, presentation, clarification, affirmation, reflection and conclusion. The

Reflecting Team model and process steps are described in more detail in Chapter Six.

Practice tips

*   Prepare yourself and the coachee well for the coaching engagement, communicating practical details and an overview of what might be expected.
*   Establish a broad vision of what the beginning, middle and end of the coaching engagement might look like.
*   Contract confidentiality and ways of working with the coaching client.
*   Observe the dynamics of the coach–client relationship, agreeing clear goals and respecting boundaries.
*   Consider your options and select a form of coaching supervision, communicating this to your coaching clients.

Discussion points

*   How important is the coach–coachee relationship in order to make progress within coaching?
*   What concerns do you have using technology as part of your solution focused coaching practice?
*   What are the key ethical issues that coaches need to consider within their practice?
*   Is supervision essential?

Suggested reading

Hawkins, P. and Smith, N. (2006) Coaching, *Mentoring and Organizational Consultancy: Supervision and Development.* Maidenhead: Open University Press.

McKergow, M. and Clarke, J. (2005) *Positive Approaches to Change: Applications of Solutions Focus and Appreciative Inquiry at Work.* Cheltenham: SolutionsBooks.

McKergow, M. and Clarke, J. (2007) *Solutions Focus Working: 80 Real Life Lessons for Successful Organisational Change.* Cheltenham: SolutionsBooks.

Palmer, S. and Panchal, S. (2011) *Developmental Coaching: Life Transitions and Generational Perspectives.* Hove: Routledge.

UKASFP (2008) *United Kingdom Association for Solution Focused Practice Code of Ethics.* London: UKASFP.

8

The inclusive coach

Few coaches would claim that any one approach works all the time. Most members of any helping or facilitative profession need to be flexible and adapt to the needs of different contexts and client groups. Many welcome anything that helps in a tight corner when everything else has failed! In this chapter we consider the different ways in which solution focused coaching may use techniques, interventions, models and theories drawn from other approaches and also summarise what solution focused coaching has to offer other coaching approaches.

An integrated approach

Proponents of solution focused coaching in its purest form do not necessarily advocate the integration of other coaching approaches into the solution focused coaching framework. These practitioners believe the very success of solution focused coaching is dependent on the model being used as it is, and in respecting the solution focused principles of:

- Keeping things simple.
- Minimising theory and concepts.
- Avoiding over-analysis of the problem.

While integration of solution focused coaching with other more theoretically based approaches may appear to go against the principles of solution focused practice, in reality both coach and coachee can handle these tensions well (O'Connell, 2005). Solution focused coaching has indeed been creatively adapted and integrated with other coaching approaches, and has been successfully applied by experienced practitioners across a range of contexts (O'Connell, 2005). Interestingly, those who advocate integration might also point to solution focused coaching principles in order to support this inclusive practice (O'Connell, 2005):

- Minimising ideology.
- Doing what works for the client.
- Doing something different.
- Being open to ideas.
- Maintaining a solution seeking mind set.

Integration of solution focused coaching with other coaching approaches might also be said to embody a solution focused view of the coaching practitioner; trusting in their unique set of strengths, skills and resources as a coach, and trusting them to draw upon this knowledge and experience to facilitate the most effective coaching solution in a given coaching engagement. In this way, the inclusive coach adopts a holistic solution focused view of the coachee, coach and coach–coachee relationship.

There are a number of ways in which solution focused coaching may be integrated with other approaches. Some practitioners view solution focused coaching as one strand of their coaching practice, to be drawn upon as appropriate to the coaching conversation and to the needs of the coachee. Arnold Lazarus referred to this practice as 'technical eclecticism' (Lazarus, 1981). Technical eclecticism may be considered consistent with the solution focused coaching principles of subscribing to minimal theory and finding the simplest route to change that works for the coachee (O'Connell, 2005). Other proponents of solution focused practice have carefully considered how solution focused coaching might be more formerly integrated with other coaching theories and models, including:

- Person-centred coaching (see O'Connell, 2005; Joseph and Jefferies, 2007; Joseph, 2010).
- Positive psychology (see Seligman, 1999; Linley and Harrington, 2007; Kauffman et al., 2010).
- Appreciative inquiry (see McKergow, 2004).

- Mindfulness (see Kabat-Zinn, 1994; Spence, 2006).
- Narrative coaching (see Drake, 2010).
- The change cycle (Prochaska and DiClemente, 1986; Prochaska *et al.*, 1992).
- Motivational interviewing (Miller and Rollnick, 2002; Passmore and Whybrow, 2007; Passmore, 2011).
- Goal theory (Latham and Locke, 1991).
- Problem solving (see Palmer, 2007).
- Multimodal models (see Lazarus, 1981; Lazarus and Abramovitz, 2004; Hutchins, 1989).
- Imagery and experiential techniques (see Palmer and Cooper, 2007; 2010).
- Cognitive behavioural coaching (see Grant, 2001).

Table 8.1 maps these coaching theories and approaches to solution focused coaching, summarising where in 'SOLUTION,' the eight-step SFC model presented in Chapter Two, different theoretical concepts and practical

Table 8.1 Integrating solution focused coaching

'SOLUTION' Model	Integration
Share updates	Appreciative Inquiry (AI); Cycle of change
Observe interests	AI; Cycle of change
Listen to hopes and goals	Person-centred; Goal theory; Imagery and experiential techniques; Multimodal; Change of cycle; Motivational Interviewing (MI); Narrative coaching; Cognitive Behavioural Coaching (CBC)
Understand exceptions	Positive psychology; AI, Multi-modal Problem solving; Narrative coaching
Tap potential	Positive psychology; AI; Imagery
Imagine success	Imagery techniques; Multi-modal coaching
Own outcomes	Experiential techniques; Multi-modal SMART objectives; Mindfulness; CBC
Note contributions	AI

coaching interventions might be introduced (see Williams *et al.*, 2011).

The remainder of this chapter will give a flavour of the different theories and approaches listed above, suggesting practical coaching interventions for use within the SOLUTION coaching model, along with recommendations for further reading should the theory or approach be of particular interest to you.

1 Person-centred coaching

The person-centred approach was originally developed by Carl Rogers, and encompasses the notion that people have the potential to self-actualise given the right social environment conditions, and that they are the expert on their own lives (Joseph and Bryant-Jefferies, 2007; Joseph, 2010). In the person-centred approach, the practitioner offers the coachee unconditional positive regard through a facilitative, non-directive questioning style. For more information on the person-centred approach see Hedman (2001) and Joseph and Bryant-Jefferies' chapter 'Person-centred coaching psychology' in *The Handbook of Coaching Psychology* (2007).

Solution focused coaching has been described as having a 'legitimate claim' to being a 'person-centred approach' (Wilkins, 1993; O'Connell, 2005). Solution focused coaching incorporates beliefs that are consistent with person-centred core values, such as respect for the autonomy of the client, disowning the role of expert and trusting the client's capability to solve their own problem (O'Connell, 2005).

Principles derived from a person-centred approach that align well with a solution focused approach include:

- Believing that the coachee is intrinsically motivated to function optimally (Joseph and Bryant-Jefferies, 2007).
- Paying attention to the social environmental conditions of the coaching engagement, acknowledging that (Rogers, 1957; Joseph and Bryant-Jefferies, 2007):
  - Your behaviour will impact the coachee's behaviour, and vice versa.

- The coachee needs to see that you have unconditional positive regard for them; to believe that they are not being judged.
- The coachee requires you to be empathic towards them and their experience.

• Believing in the self-determination of the coachee, and as such adopting a non-directive coaching style.

2 Positive psychology

The positive psychology movement has grown exponentially since Martin Seligman highlighted the need to shift the psychology's focus from understanding mental illness to understanding health, well-being and performance (see Seligman, 1999). Positive psychology has been described as the 'science of optimal human functioning ... [with] ... research topics including happiness, wisdom, creativity and human strengths' (Linley and Harrington, 2007: 42). For more information visit Martin Seligman's 'Authentic happiness' website www.authentichappiness.sas.upenn.edu/Default.aspx.

Positive psychology and solution focused coaching have much in common, both being forward-looking with an emphasis on identification and utilisation of natural strengths, visualisation of a preferred future and achievement of desired goals. Positive psychology interventions that may benefit the solution focused practitioner during the steps of 'Understand exceptions' and 'Tap potential' of the SOLUTION model include the following.

• *Three good things* In this established positive psychology exercise the coachee is encouraged to reflect nightly on three things that went well during the day (Kauffman, Boniwell and Silberman, 2010). The intention is to encourage a positive bias in memory, and the positive effects on happiness levels are well documented. A solution focused adaptation of this exercise might be to ask the question in the context of a past success: 'What three good things happened?' 'What three things did you do well to make that a success?'

- *Strengths based questionnaires* The VIA survey of strengths (Peterson and Seligman, 2004) is available free online at www.authentichappiness.sas.upenn.edu/Default.aspx and can be a very powerful way of profiling the coaches' signature strengths. An alternative questionnaire, Realise2, is available from the Centre for Applied Positive Psychology's (Linley, Willars and Biswas-Diener, 2010). For more information visit www.cappeu.com/Realise2.aspx.
- *The concept of FLOW* (Csíkszentmihályi, 1998) In Chapter Three we mentioned the concept of being in 'flow,' or 'in the zone' (Csíkszentmihályi, 1998), which enables individuals to focus on the task and maximise performance (Wesson and Boniwell, 2007). Invite the coachee to think of a time when they were fully in the moment and absorbed in what they were doing: what was the context; how were they behaving, thinking and feeling; what might they learn from this experience that might be transferred to the current situation; what might need to be different for them to take a step towards being in flow with their current challenge?
- *Savouring positive experiences* (Kauffman *et al.*, 2010) Invite the coachee to reflect on specific positive experiences in their daily lives, and to appreciatively review these experiences (see Kauffman *et al.*, 2010).

3 Appreciative inquiry

Appreciative Inquiry (AI) grew from the work of David Cooperrider and Suresh Srivastva (Cooperrider 1986; Cooperrider and Srivastva, 1987) and 'is about the co-evolutionary search for the best in people, their organizations, and the relevant world around them ... AI involves, in a central way, the art and practice of asking questions that strengthen a system's capacity to apprehend, anticipate, and heighten positive potential' (Cooperrider and Whitney, 2004: 3). AI is traditionally applied at a group and organisational level, although many of its principles and practices may be usefully adapted for individual clients.

While Appreciative Inquiry and solution focused coaching have evolved independently, they appear to share many underlying principles, values and aspirations. The

Appreciative Inquiry 4-D model (Cooperrider and Whitney, 1999) describes the four key stages of Discovery (appreciating the best of the individual, team and organisation), Dream (visualising the possibilities), Design (co-constructing the ideal state or goal) and Destiny (maintaining the ideal state or goal); strongly echoing the strengths-seeking, visualisation of preferred futures and goal focus aspects of the SFC approach. For more information see the work of Cooperrider and Whitney (1999), as well as McKergow and Clarke's (Eds) (2005) *Positive Approaches to Change: Applications of Solutions Focus and Appreciative Inquiry at Work.*

Engaging in the AI practice of listening for and reinforcing the coachee's strengths and resources will be instrumental to the solution focused practitioner and their client throughout a solution focused coaching session. The following AI-based coaching interventions may be of particular use in the SOLUTION model under 'Share updates,' 'Observe interests,' 'Understand exceptions' and 'Tap potential':

- *Affirmative topic choice* Invite the coachee to choose the topic of the coaching conversation: 'what is it that you want to learn or achieve?' (Cooperrider and Whitney, 2004: 5).
- *The 'spirit of inquiry'* (Cooperrider and Whitney, 2004) The aim of this exercise is to discover the individual, team or organisations' potential to change. Invite the coachee to share stories of when they have been at their best; explore 'every strength, innovation, achievement, resource, living value, imaginative story, benchmark, hope, positive tradition, passion, high point experience, internal genius, dream' (Cooperrider and Whitney, 2004: 7).
- *Internal others* (McNamee, 2004) This exercise is adapted from McNamee's (2004) concept of 'Internal others.' Invite the coachee to reflect on a successful past experience, and to talk appreciatively from a number of different perspectives – what would their manager have said they did well; their peers and colleagues; their partner and so on; what strengths would each person have seen them utilise; how might these strengths and resources be beneficial to them now to achieve their present goal?

- *From Discovery to Dream* In AI, the insights gathered from the inquiry stage are then translated in to the dream (Cooperrider and Whitney, 2004); what does the coachee dream of achieving; what does their preferred future look like?
- *Creating the Ideal* Once the dream has been visualised, help the coachee to identify the strengths, skills and resources they have to make this dream a reality; how can they use the best of 'what is' to take positive steps towards 'what might be' (Cooperrider and Whitney, 2004); what needs to be different in order to achieve this vision?
- *Achieve your Destiny* The final stage of the AI 4D's model is about more than delivering change; it is about the coachee achieving and maintaining their state of 'flow' (Csíkszentmihályi, 1998); utilising their signature strengths to achieve the desired goal and desired future state; in Cooperrider and Whitney's words, it is about achieving one's destiny (Cooperrider and Whitney, 2004). In practical terms, within a solution focused approach, this may take the form of a 'notice assignment,' in which the coachee observes how and when they have made positive progress towards their goal; what it feels like to have achieved these positive changes; what strengths and resources they are drawing on to sustain these achievements; how it feels to be doing what they were meant to be doing.

4 Mindfulness

Kabat-Zinn's (1994) book *Wherever You Go, There You Are* provides powerful insights in to mindfulness and how the simple art of meditation may be instrumental to us (and our coachees) in our daily lives. He describes mindfulness as an ancient Buddhist practice that is about being aware that we can live our life without actually being in the moment, mindlessly completing our daily tasks. Mindfulness is 'the art of conscious living' (Kabat-Zinn, 1994: 6) and is about 'being in touch with this not-knowing' (Kabat-Zinn, 1994: xiii). At its core mindfulness is about focusing attention, heightening awareness, focusing on the present and accepting what is (Kabat-Zinn, 1994; Segal, Williams and Teasdale, 2002; Passmore and Marianetti, 2007).

In order to strive towards achieving a goal, one needs to remain focused on that goal, and in this way the concept of mindfulness is highly relevant in coaching (Spence, 2006). Kabat-Zinn describes some of the basic principles of mindfulness (Kabat-Zinn, 1994), which closely echo the intentions of solution focused coaching:

- Purposeful attention.
- Being present in the moment.
- Non-judgemental self-observation.
- Appreciation of what is.
- Mindful action.

Whilst meditation on internal states is the most established route to mindfulness, alternative routes include socio-cognitive awareness through creative thinking and non-judgemental observation of the external environment, and depersonalisation through detached mindfulness of the external environment (Spence, 2006). For more information see details of established mindfulness-based programmes as follows:

- Mindfulness-based meditation programmes (Kabat-Zinn, 1990).
- Mindfulness-based cognitive therapy (Teasdale, 2004).
- Acceptance and commitment therapy (Hayes and Wilson, 2003).
- Dialectical Behavior Therapy (DBT) (Linehan, Cochran and Kehrer, 2001).

The efficacy of mindfulness and mindfulness training has been researched in recent years, particularly in combination with cognitive-behavioural, solution focused (CB-SF) coaching:

- Spence (2006) researched the impact of mindfulness training in advance of CB-SF coaching, and found it facilitated the attainment of health goals by helping people prepare for change (Spence, 2006).
- Spence, Cavanagh and Grant (2008) researched mindfulness training and CB-SF coaching and found that participants receiving coaching showed significantly greater

goal attainment in comparison to a group receiving a series of health education seminars.

• Collard and Walsh (2008) researched their Sensory Awareness Mindfulness Training (SAMT) and found improvements in mood and reductions in stress levels.

According to this research, mindfulness-based coaching interventions may be most beneficial prior to solution focused, cognitive-behavioural (SF-CB) coaching, training the coachee in the concepts and skills of mindfulness (Spence, 2006). The coachee may then be reminded to be mindful when going about their in-between session tasks, for example completing notice assignments in a non-judgemental way.

The following mindfulness-based coaching interventions may be useful prior to or during a solution focused coaching session based on the SOLUTION model:

• *Breathing exercises* Breathing provides an ideal anchor when we are seeking to quieten our inner voices (Kabat-Zinn, 1994). Kabat-Zinn (1994) suggests simply focusing on how it feels to breathe in and out, as a way of shifting your attention back to the present moment.
• *Non-judgemental observation* The concept of non-judgemental observation is fundamental to solution focused coaching. Encourage the coachee to be more compassionate towards him/herself, observing events and their reactions to events while withholding judgement, thereby collecting useful insights and empowering him/herself to make clearer, more informed choices in the future.
• *Daily practice of mindfulness attention* The beauty of mindfulness is that it can be practised for short or long periods of time, at any time. The coachee may be encouraged to practise completing small daily tasks mindfully, whether brushing their teeth, eating food or completing a task at work.
• *Detecting novelty* This exercise is intended to help the coachee mindfully attend to what is different and new (Langer, 1994). Encourage the coachee to see the problem from different perspectives, increasing the likelihood of novel thoughts and experiences.

- *Physical activities* Physical activities such as yoga, walking, martial arts, movement and dance are all highly effective ways in which mindfulness may be practiced (Anderson, 2009).

5 The narrative approach

Narrative coaching works on the premise that the way people narrate their lives impacts upon their behaviour (Drake, 2010). The goal of narrative coaching is to help the coachee embrace any current conflict and to truly understand it, in order to facilitate a move beyond it (Drake, 2010).

While solution focused coaching focuses on the future, it is still useful and important to retrieve transferable skills from the person's past experience. Narrative coaching approaches can help the coachee to understand the scripts of their past, identifying what is part of the problem and what part of the solution. As we noted in Chapter Five, it is through the telling and re-shaping of their story that truths emerge for the coachee. This is in accordance with the solution focused coaching principle of problem-talk; of listening to the coachee talk through the problem for as long as they need in order to validate their concerns in readiness to change. It is useful to draw attention to the stories frequently told by the coachee, as well as their 'latent potential stories' (Drake, 2007); the stories they don't but could tell themselves, that would be helpful to their current self-description (Drake, 2007). For more information on the narrative coaching approach see Drake (2010).

The following two narrative-based coaching interventions may be integrated within the SOLUTION model at the steps of 'Listen to hopes and goals' and 'Understand exceptions':

- *Questions for exploring narrative* Burke (1969) identified six key questions for understanding a story: what was done, when and where did it happen, who did it, how did he do it and why.
- *Storyboard exercise* Invite the coachee to create a storyboard of their past, present or anticipated future

experience. Listen for what is included in the story, and for what is not (Drake, 2010); what are they trying to accomplish with their current story (Drake, 2010); what part of the story is open to challenge or re-definition; what different perspectives can they tell their story from? (Freedman and Combs, 1996). This exercise may also be usefully adapted for exploring the preferred future vision.

6 The cycle of change

While some coachees begin a coaching engagement highly motivated to change their situation or problem, for others it may not be that simple. Some may see the need to change but feel blocked to act, while some may actually feel strong resistance against the coaching process, particularly if they believe they are not there by their own volition. De Shazer (1988) describes the different agendas of the Visitor, Complainant and Customer. The visitor doesn't think he has a problem and/or doesn't want to be coached; the complainant recognises he has a problem but does not want to be coached; the customer recognises he has a problem and views the coaching process as a way of finding potential solutions (de Shazer, 1988; O'Connell, 2005). There may be a number of reasons why the coachee is resistant of the coaching process, such as lack of knowledge, awareness, motivation or social skills to move the problem forward (O'Connell, 2005).

A well-known model of change is Prochaska and DiClemente's 'Transtheoretical Model of Change' (Prochaska and DiClemente, 1986; Prochaska, DiClemente and Norcross, 1992), which recognises five key stages of Pre-contemplation, Contemplation, Preparation, Action and Maintenance with a sixth stage relating to Relapse:

1 *Pre-contemplation* The reluctant coachee with little or no intrinsic motivation.
2 *Contemplation* The coachee who wants to change but does not know how to.
3 *Preparation* The coachee who has made some decisions and is making plans.

4 *Action* The coachee who has already taken steps towards achieving their goal.
5 *Maintenance* The coachee who has successfully implemented their changes, but who may feel the need to consciously monitor their behaviour, and may need coping strategies should they relapse to earlier stages of the cycle.
6 *Relapse* The coachee may lapse due to internal and/or external factors.

This framework can be instrumental when assessing the coachee's readiness for change. Progress through the change model is not always linear, and as such the coach or coachee may observe that the coachee is re-visiting an earlier stage, or is finding themself stuck in a particular stage for a long time (O'Connell, 2005). Palmer (2011a) illustrates the type of coachee dialogue at each stage in Figure 8.1.

Using the models described above, the coach may understand the coachee's stage of change and ensure that they are

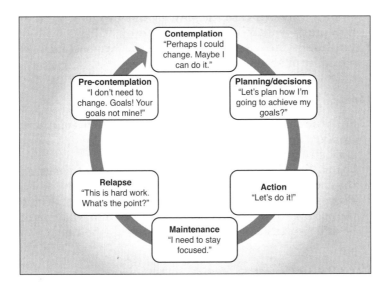

Figure 8.1 Transtheoretical model or stages of change model (after Prochaska & DiClemente, 1982) (Palmer, 2011a)

not rushed too quickly into identification of solutions (Greene and Grant, 2003; O'Connell, 2005). If the coachee is rushed, the coaching may be experienced as 'solution-forced' (Nylund and Corsiglia, 1994) rather than 'solution-focused.' For more information see Prochaska and associates' (1992) article 'In search of how people change.'

The following coaching interventions are informed by these models of change and have been adapted from O'Connell (2005). They may be useful at the earlier steps of the SOLUTION model of 'Share updates,' 'Observe interests' and 'Listen to hopes and goals.'

Pre-contemplation/visitor

- Stay with problem-talk for as long as the coachee needs. Listening to their problem will help to validate their perception of the situation.
- Be accepting of their ambivalence, and avoid arguing for change.
- Ask the coachee what they want to ensure they *don't* change; this can ease the way for them to look at what they might want to change (O'Connell, 2005).
- Encourage the coachee to imagine the circumstances in which he or she might want to change.

Contemplation/complainant

- Shift the emphasis from the problem to possible solutions; from the past to the future.
- Seek strengths, resources and exceptions.
- Utilise the Miracle Question (de Shazer, 1988) to imagine the coachee's preferred future.
- Propose 'notice' assignments in-between meetings, to help the coachee observe what is working well and what might be different to achieve small steps towards their goal.

Preparation

- Set clear, realistic and attainable goals.
- Utilise strengths, resources and signature solutions.

- Propose 'Pretend' and 'Do something different' assignments.

Action/customer

- Encourage the client to keep doing what is working.
- Reinforce constructive change by reflecting this back to the coachee.
- Provide positive feedback on the client's proactive contributions and readiness for change.

Maintenance

- Normalise the possibility of relapse, highlight that the right contextual cues might trigger this for any person and plan for such an occurrence.
- Explain the concept of non-judgemental observation and recommend 'Notice assignments.'
- Continue to seek exceptions; what was the client doing at the times when they were not relapsing? What strengths, skills and resources were they utilising at this time? What was different about the situation and environment?
- Explore 'solution focused force-field analysis' questions with the coachee (see O'Connell, 2005): when, where and how might obstacles arise; what will be the first signs that you've met an obstacle; what have you learned from past experiences where you have successfully overcome these challenges?

Relapse

- Reframe relapse as a lapse, e.g. just because you have lapsed today on maintaining some target does not mean that it's a total relapse.
- As previously, normalise relapse. As fallible human beings we may relapse under stress and pressure (N.B. Boredom can also lead to stress which can trigger comfort eating and drinking which needs to be noted if undertaking solution focused health coaching).

- During this recent 'lapse' are there any exceptions?
- Recall what has previously worked. Can it be applied again?

7 Motivational interviewing

Motivational Interviewing (MI) is an approach originally developed by William Miller and Steve Rollnick to help clients overcome resistance to their own goals by highlighting and enhancing intrinsic motivation (Miller and Rollnick, 2002; Passmore and Whybrow, 2007). Miller and Rollnick assert that Motivational Interviewing is a collaborative, person-centred form of guiding to elicit and strengthen motivation for change (Miller and Rollnick, 2009: 137).

Principles of MI that align well to solution focused coaching include respecting the individual's choice and control, adopting a collaborative, non-directive style and engaging in active listening (Passmore and Whybrow, 2007). An MI coach respects the coachee, values their autonomy and believes in their potential (Miller and Rollnick, 2002). For more information see Miller and Rollnick's (2002) book *Motivational Interviewing: Preparing People for Change*, and Passmore and Whybrow's (2007) chapter 'Motivational Interviewing: A specific approach for coaching psychologists.'

Motivational Interviewing techniques may be particularly useful at the third step of the SOLUTION model, 'Listening to hopes and goals.' Solution focused health coaching often benefits from the use of motivational interviewing techniques especially at the pre-contemplative stage. Practical interventions that may be integrated into the solution focused approach include the following.

- *Assessing readiness to change* Explore the coachee's readiness to change using the solution focused coaching scaling technique – on a scale of zero to ten, where ten is they have already made change and zero is no interest in changing (Passmore and Whybrow, 2007; Passmore, 2011).
- *Active listening* Listen carefully to the coachee to understand their view of the problem, options available and

what has been planned and executed so far (Passmore, 2011).

- *Personal profiling* Describe their values, ideals, and ideal future self; this exercise is aimed at shifting the coachee's focus from the current negative situation or problem to a more positive future (Passmore and Whybrow, 2007).
- *Develop discrepancy* People need to see the change as in line with their values, and of value to them (Miller and Rollnick, 2002). Invite the coachee to describe their current and ideal selves (Passmore and Whybrow, 2007); use open questions to highlight how current goal-blocking behaviours may not be aligned to their values and ideals (Miller and Rollnick, 2002).
- *The language of change* Miller and Rollnick (2002) coined the term 'change talk,' describing a continuum on which people differ in terms of their readiness to change. Describe the continuum from one, where the individual is focused on and talking about the current problem to ten, where the individual is focused on and stating a clear intention to change. Help the coachee to increase their change talk by asking where on the scale they are currently, and what would it take for them to move along the scale (Passmore and Whybrow, 2007).
- *The confidence ruler* (Passmore and Whybrow, 2007) Use the scaling question to explore the coachee's confidence to change: On a scale of zero to ten where one is low confidence and ten is high confidence, how confident are they that they can achieve this change; what does it feel like to be where they are on the scale; what would it look like if they were at a six or seven on the scale; what small step could they take to move one notch up this scale?

8 Goal theory

Goal development is an important part of the solution focused coaching process, and has been found to be fundamental for self-regulated behaviour (Bandura, 1986; Grant, 2001); as a general rule, people behave in a more disciplined way when they have a challenging, specific and attainable goal in mind (Latham and Locke, 1991). Goal theory was advanced by

Edwin Locke and Gary Latham (1990), and led to widespread use of goal-setting techniques in the workplace (Locke and Latham, 1984; 2005). Their theory has been integrated into many coaching frameworks, where the coachee is asked to identify and work towards Specific, Measurable, Achievable, Relevant and Time-bound (SMART) goals.

The act of goal-setting has been found to enhance motivation by directing the person's attention, mobilising their efforts and encouraging task persistence (Locke, Shaw, Saari and Latham, 1981). Performance is dependent upon the individual's ability to complete the task, their belief in whether or not they are able to complete the task (their self-efficacy), and the extent to which they see the task as a personal, as opposed to assigned, goal (Locke and Latham, 1990). The two-stage theory of goal-setting proposes that people first form intentions to act if they perceive the outcome worthwhile (Heckhausen and Kuhl, 1985), but only enter the goal-striving phase if they believe it viable given personal and situational constraints (Gollwitzer, 1990).

Goal-focused questions that may be useful within the SOLUTION model step of 'Listen to hopes and goals' include:

- How will you know that coming here today has been helpful?
- What would you like to achieve?
- What would you like to change?
- What needs to change?
- What will be the first signs that things are improving?

9 From problem solving to solution seeking

In their life coaching book, Neenan and Dryden describe a problem as being practical and/or emotional in nature and as being 'a present state of facing a particular difficulty without having found an effective solution' (Neenan and Dryden, 2002: 26). Wasik (1984) developed a seven-step problem solving framework, which Palmer adapted to provide the useful 'PRACTICE' acronym for coaching (Palmer, 2007; 2008b; 2011b), as follows:

Purpose of coaching programme (or Problem identification
or Preferred Outcome or Preferred Options)
Realistic, relevant goals developed
Alternative solution(s) generated
Consideration of consequences
Target most feasible solution(s)
Implementation of
Chosen solution(s)
Evaluation

The PRACTICE model began as a problem-solving framework (Palmer 2007) and the 'P' initially represented 'Problem
identification.' Over time the model evolved into a solution
focused framework, with the inclusion of SF techniques such
as problem-free talk, scaling questions, exception seeking
and solution-seeking (Palmer, 2008b). Later Palmer (2011b)
suggested that on some occasions when the coachee is unsure
of the problem or has fuzzy and unspecific goals, it can be
advantageous initially to discuss or explore the purpose of
their coaching programme instead of focusing on problem
identification. For example, a coachee may want a career
change but has no clear vision of which new path to take. Yet
on other occasions, a coachee can quite quickly see 'Preferred
options' or 'Preferred outcomes' and problem identification
is less relevant. Therefore the PRACTICE model can be flexibly adapted and applied by the coach according to what
issues the coachee brings to the first session.

Coachees often find it really useful to use the PRACTICE
worksheet, which can be completed during the coaching
session with the assistance of the coach (see Appendix 2).
They can then use the form to aid self-coaching outside of
the coaching session. Cognitive techniques may also be
effectively integrated in to the PRACTICE framework as
and when the coachee appears blocked by unhelpful or
performance interfering thoughts (PITs) (e.g. 'I can't do it')
or feelings (e.g. Anxiety) (see Palmer, 2007; 2008b). The
framework has been adapted to other languages and cultures
(e.g. Dias, Gandos, Nardi and Palmer, 2011) and has also
been used within business coaching (Williams, Palmer and
Wallace 2011). (For more background information, see
Palmer, 2007; 2008b; 2011b.)

Two further techniques that may be useful during the 'Listen to hopes and goals' step of the SOLUTION model are as follows.

- *In a word* If the coachee is experiencing difficulty concisely explaining the problem, Lazarus (1981) recommends asking the client to describe the problem in one word, and then that one word is put into one sentence. Then sometimes it is useful for the person to expand on that one sentence and include it in one paragraph. This can be a very powerful tool for focusing attention prior to formulation of the coaching goal. Interestingly, the one word that a coachee may often express is an emotion such as 'anxious.' Let's take one example: a) Anxious b) I'm anxious about giving a presentation c) I'm anxious about giving a presentation at work to the board of directors. If I screw it up I may wreck my chances of promotion. After all the hard work I've done too.
- *SF force-field analysis* Force-field analysis may be utilised to help the coachee understand what is helping and hindering them from achieving their goal (Egan, 1990). Once they have generated a list of restraining and facilitating forces, they may then explore ways to 'do something different,' by maximising the positives and minimising the negatives (O'Connell, 2005).

10 Multimodal models

Arnold Lazarus (1981; 1989) developed the multimodal approach, recognising the role of behaviour, affect, sensation, imagery, cognition, interpersonal relationships and drugs/biological factors in his 'BASIC ID' framework (Lazarus, 1981; Lazarus and Abramovitz, 2004). Other multimodal coaching models and frameworks available include SPACE (Social context, Physical reaction, Action, Cognition, Emotion: Edgerton and Palmer, 2005) and CLARITY (Context, Life event, Action, Reaction, Imagery, Thoughts, Your choice: Williams and Palmer, 2010). Multimodal models are used in coaching to help the coachee fully understand a positive or negative experience, to challenge elements within this, and to generate alternative ways of thinking, emotionally feeling, imagining, sensing, relating to others and behaving (Palmer, 2008a).

Hutchins' (1989) TFA model highlights the different modes of language and perception: Thinking, Feeling and Acting. Each person tends to have a dominant mode that they use automatically, and often subconsciously. For example, a coachee may frequently describe what they think of events, but rarely refer to how they feel about events, or vice versa. Hutchins recommends matching your coachee's language and building on their TFA strengths (Hutchins, 1989); if the coachee tends to describe what they think, as coach you may choose to reflect back what you think, rather than saying 'I feel.'

For more information see Palmer's (2008a) article 'Multimodal coaching and its application to the workplace, life and health coaching.'

Coaching interventions informed by the multimodal approach may be utilised within the SOLUTION model in the steps of 'Understand exceptions,' 'Listen to hopes and goals,' 'Imagine success' and 'Own outcomes':

- *Understanding exceptions* Multimodal models may be used to help the coachee explore a past, present or antici- pated future event in detail; in the moment, what are they thinking, feeling, doing (Edgerton and Palmer, 2005); what is the evidence for/against any unhelpful reactions; what might be a more helpful reaction; how might these insights help them in their current situation?
- *Overcoming barriers to change* Multimodal models may be used to overcome cognitive and emotional barriers to change. For more details on how each model might be used see the relevant articles listed above.
- *PITs and PETs* (Palmer, 2003) Encourage the coachee to write down any Performance Interfering Thoughts (PITs), and to generate replacement Performance Enhancing Thoughts (PETs).
- *Imagine success* Multimodal models may be used to help the coachee build a robust image of the preferred future.

11 Imagery and experiential techniques

Imagery techniques invite the coachee to visualise different versions of events; experiential techniques invite the coachee to have an actual experience. Both techniques have been found to be extremely effective. Imagery forms an essential part of the solution focused coaching process tapped into by the Miracle Question (de Shazer, 1988) and the development of a preferred future vision. For some individuals, non-verbal, experiential activities such as role-play or drawing may help to access feelings and emotions not readily accessible to them through verbal discussion (O'Connell, 2005). Bischof (1993) encourages clients to act out exceptions and preferred future visions.

The following coaching interventions may be useful at the 'Listen to hopes and goals,' 'Tap potential' and 'Imagine success' steps of the SOLUTION model:

- *Self-motivation imagery* (Palmer and Cooper, 2007; 2010) Self-motivation imagery involves asking the coachee to first imagine what life will be like if they never achieve their goal: what is the impact on themselves and significant others; what are they doing and how are they feeling; what regrets do they have? Then ask the coachee to imagine they have achieved their goal: what are they doing and how are they feeling; what is the impact on themselves and others; what are the benefits of this change for themselves and others? Finally ask the coachee to compare these two images and the extent to which they feel motivated to take steps towards achieving their goal (scaling may be useful here).
- *Scaling walk* In Chapter Nine we describe a 'scaling walk' exercise in which coachees are invited to physically step onto a line of numbers one to ten, and to describe where they are, before moving to stand on and describe where they would like to be.
- *Sketch it* Invite the coachee to draw strip cartoons (O'Connell, 2005) of the perceived problem, a previous success or a preferred future vision. Talk through the themes and meanings that arise, highlighting strengths, resources and signature solutions.
- *Compassion-focused imagery* (Palmer, 2009) If the coachee is particularly self-critical, a compassion-focused imagery

exercise might be beneficial. Invite the coachee to visualise being in receipt of compassion from an external source, really imagining what it feels like to receive this compassion. Encourage the coachee to maintain this vision through practice.

- *Time-projection imagery* (Palmer, 2008a) Sometimes known as 'time tripping' (Lazarus, 1981), time-projection imagery may be used to help the coachee regain perspective and reduce stress levels. Invite the coachee to picture themselves in three months, six months, twelve months, two years, five years' time, and to consider whether the current problem will seem as stressful, and to what extent they can see themselves getting on with their lives (Palmer and Cooper, 2007; 2010).
- *Book of solutions* (O'Connell, 2005) Coachees may find it useful to non-judgementally observe and note down solutions that they use on a day-to-day basis. This book of solutions may be reviewed in the coaching session to identify any themes or signature solutions.
- *Coping imagery* (Palmer and Cooper, 2007; 2010) Coping imagery, or goal-rehearsal imagery, is where the coachee visualises themselves dealing with the problem, and may be highly effective if the coachee appears to be stressed about events (Lazarus, 1981; Palmer and Cooper, 2007; 2010). Discuss the feared situation with the coachee and encourage them to think of different ways in which they might cope with it. Invite the coachee to imagine him/ herself in the feared situation, and imagine them coping with it, repeating this imagery recall several times. Encourage the coachee to practice the imagery in-between sessions to strengthen its impact and prepare for the anticipated situation (Palmer and Cooper, 2007; 2010).

12 Cognitive behavioural techniques and interventions

Cognitive behavioural techniques and interventions help the coachee to understand how negative self-talk might be influencing how they feel about a situation and how they choose to behave (Neenan and Dryden, 2002). Aaron T. Beck first coined the phrase 'internal dialogue' (Beck, 1976) to describe the critical inner voice that makes us question our self-efficacy and self-worth (Williams, Edgerton and Palmer, 2010). Albert Ellis (1962) recognised the role of emotional disturbance in determining actions – in his 'ABC' model the link between Activating event and its Consequences is mediated by the person's self-limiting Beliefs about the event and their ability to handle it (see Ellis, 1994).

The theory and practice of cognitive behavioural coaching grew from cognitive behavioural therapy, possibly one of the most researched therapeutic approaches available. A number of common thinking errors have been identified, including mind-reading, making unrealistic demands, globally labelling oneself as a 'failure' or 'useless' and procrastinating based on the belief that 'I can't stand it' (Palmer and Szymanska, 2007). For more information on the CBC approach see Neenan and Dryden's (2002).

Grant describes how solution focused techniques make the more clinically derived CBC techniques both accessible and acceptable to non-clinical coaching clients (Grant, 2001). The integration of solution focused coaching and cognitive behavioural coaching is perhaps the best researched and evidenced of all the solution focused coaching integrations, and demonstrates that combining these approaches can be to the benefit of the coachee (Palmer, Grant and O'Connell, 2007). Research has shown that coaching with a solution focused, cognitive behavioural model (SF-CB) can enhance goal striving and attainment (Grant, 2001; Green et al., 2006; Spence and Grant, 2007; Yu et al., 2008; Grant et al., 2009), life satisfaction (Grant, 2001; Spence and Grant, 2007), resilience (Green et al., 2007; Grant, 2008; Grant et al., 2009), and hope (Green et al., 2007), and can reduced stress, anxiety and depression (Green et al., 2007; Grant, 2008; Grant et al., 2009).

Cognitive behavioural techniques and interventions may be useful at any stage in solution focused coaching, as and when the coach becomes aware of the presence of negative self-talk that is preventing the coachee from progressing with their search for solutions. It is most likely to fit into the SOLUTION model during the steps of 'Listening for hopes and goals' and later at 'Owning outcomes.' The following cognitive behavioural coaching techniques may be of use.

- *Examining beliefs* Listen to old beliefs and invite the coachee to rate on a scale of zero to one hundred how strongly they hold this belief; help the coachee to formulate a non-problematic version of this belief; encourage the coachee to search for evidence that supports the new belief, or disputes the old belief; continue to rate both beliefs until the new belief is stronger than the old one (see O'Connell, 2005).
- *Errors in thinking* Share the concept of thinking errors with the coachee (see Neenan and Dryden, 2002); identify any thinking errors that are reinforcing the problem, such as discounting the positives or over-generalising, and encourage more flexible thinking (O'Connell, 2005); suggest 'notice assignments' whereby the coachee observes, without judgement, when unhelpful thoughts are blocking their progress, and how they manage to overcome this challenge.
- *Perspective* Help the coachee to regain perspective. Ask the coachee to rate the problem on a scale of zero to ten, where one is not problematic and ten is extremely problematic; ask 'If X were to be true, would it really be the end of the world?'; ask the coachee to re-rate the extent of the problem.
- *Imperative to preference* Help the coachee to recognise self-imposed demands or rules, replacing imperatives with preferences (Ellis and Blum, 1967; Palmer and Cooper, 2007; 2010).
- *Overcome procrastination* As described in Chapter Three, suggest to the coachee that they might overcome procrastination by making a start and seeing what happens!
- *Book of solutions* (O'Connell, 2005) Invite the coachee to keep a book of solutions or 'solutions journal' (O'Connell, 2005), recording times when they achieve the desired behaviour. Ask the coachee to describe the situation; what were they thinking at the time; how did they overcome any self-limiting beliefs; what do they learn from this?

- *Self-acceptance* (Palmer and Cooper, 2007; 2010) Share the concept of 'self-acceptance,' the idea of accepting oneself (and others) as fallible human beings while holding a desire (but not an imperative) to improve (Palmer and Cooper, 2007; 2010). Encourage the coachee to evaluate only specific aspects of themselves or their performance, as opposed to their whole self. For example, 'Although I failed my exam it does not make me a failure' instead of, 'I failed my exam therefore I'm a total failure as a person.'

Caveat: It is important to realise that these cognitive behavioural techniques need to be judiciously applied within solution focused coaching in order not to dilute the underlying philosophy of solution focused practice. Techniques can be applied without necessarily applying the underlying theory.

What the solution focused approach can do for other coaching approaches

What does the solution focused approach bring to the table?

1 It challenges coaches to redress the balance between problem exploration and solution construction. Techniques such as scaling and the Miracle Question (de Shazer, 1988) help to free the coachee from a preoccupation with barriers, difficulties or problems.
2 Being curious about the coachee's solution-finding strategies ensures that they are not underestimated and that due regard is given to their strengths and qualities. It encourages the coach to look for those sparks of ingenuity and improvisation unique to their coachees. It particularly challenges the coaches to trust and respect their coachees.
3 It reminds coaches that the past is not always a good indicator of future achievement. It directs attention away from reputation and labels to concentrate more on potential and future goals.
4 It highlights the importance of language in shaping realities. Careful observation ('extreme listening') of coachees'

world views as revealed in their use of language and the 'possibility-laced' language of the coach enables a shift to take place in the coachee's mind set and behaviour.

5 It pays particular attention to the context in which coachees operate and gives them the space to discover what works for them in their own particular circumstances.

6 It puts the coachee centre stage in terms of customising meetings. By staying close to the coachee's agenda and checking progress during sessions, the coach demonstrates that the key factor in facilitating change and achieving goals is the coachee.

7 It is an effective antidote to a coachee becoming dependent as it highlights the coachee's accountability and any credit for success is directly traceable to the coachee's efforts, not the skill of the coach.

Practice tips

• Develop your own inclusive, integrated model acknowledging your coaching knowledge, skills and abilities.
• Work within your own coaching capabilities.
• Actively listen to the coachee and respect their autonomy.
• Trust you will know the tools to include in the moment.
• Remain person-centred, flexible and led by the coachee.
• Integrate techniques but do not neglect the basic philosophy of the solution focused practice.
• Apply solution focused coaching principles to your own learning and development as a coach!

Discussion points

• To what extent is it appropriate to integrate the solution focused approach with other coaching psychology approaches, models, tools and techniques?
• If practising using an integrated solution focused coaching model, to what extent is this technical eclecticism or a scientifically researched and evidence-based integration?
• If advocating the integration of solution focused coaching, what other approaches, models, tools and techniques might solution focused coaching be effectively combined

with? Where have you done this already? What does or might this look like in terms of a coaching model?
- In what other contexts might an integrated solution focused coaching model be useful?

Suggested reading

Berg, I.K. and Szabó, P. (2005) *Brief Coaching for Lasting Solutions*. New York: Norton.

Locke, E.A. and Latham, G.P. (2005) Goal setting theory: Theory building by induction. In K. Smith and M. Hitt (Eds) *Great Minds in Management*. New York: Oxford University Press.

Neenan, M. and Dryden, W. (2002) *Life Coaching: A Cognitive Behavioural Perspective*. Hove: Routledge.

Palmer, S. (2008) The PRACTICE model of coaching: Towards a solution focused approach. *Coaching Psychology International*, *1*(1): 4–8.

Palmer, S. and Burton, T. (1996) *Dealing with People Problems at Work*. Berkshire: McGraw-Hill Publishing.

Palmer, S. and Cooper, C. (2007; 2010) *How to Deal with Stress*. London: Kogan-Page.

Palmer, S. and Szymanska, K. (2007) Cognitive Behavioural Coaching: An integrative approach. In S. Palmer and A. Whybrow (Eds) *Handbook of Coaching Psychology: A Guide for Practitioners*, pp.86–117. Hove: Routledge.

9

Solution focused coaching exercises

One of the defining characteristics of the solution focused community is its generosity in sharing ideas and good practice. Steve de Shazer and Insoo Kim Berg, two key founders, embodied this spirit of collective wisdom. A second characteristic of many solution focused practitioners is their creative use of the basic tools. New questions or ways of approaching a solution are constantly being tried and tested by front line workers who report back to the wider community what did or did not work with their coachees or clients.

It is in this spirit that we offer the reader a selection of exercises, which can be used with coachees or with trainees in workshops. We do not claim to be their author. Where possible, sources are acknowledged. Others we have encountered, in one form or another, on courses or at conferences. Some we will have modified, and one or two we might even have invented ourselves! To all the colleagues who have contributed directly or indirectly to this collection, we offer our warmest thanks.

The following exercises can be used in one-to-one coaching, group coaching or in workshops.

1 One small step

This is a description of the use of the exercise being with a group.

The group coach or facilitator invites everyone to draw a vertical line down the middle of a blank piece of paper. On the *left* hand side of the line the facilitator asks each person to write down a problem they currently have at work or in another area of their life.

Next the coach or facilitator asks them to write down on the *right* hand side of the line *one small step* they could take in the next few weeks that would begin to resolve the problem. This small step may not be the whole solution, but it would constitute progress. The small step must be something that *they* can do and which is not reliant upon someone else's behaviour.

The coach or facilitator then invites the group to hold up the piece of paper with the problem on it. When all have done so, the facilitator states that, 'You might be concentrating too much on the problem and it's stopping you doing anything about it.' The facilitator invites the group to rip up or discard their problem pieces of paper. The facilitator then asks them to hold up the paper with the small step written on it and states, 'But you *can* do something about this.'

The facilitator then invites them to share their 'small step' with one other person in the group. They can use the questions below to explore the small step.

- What will be the benefits to you when you take this step?
- Will there be a benefit to anyone else?
- How much effort will it take on your part?
- Is there anyone who could help you with this?
- When will you know you are ready to do it?
- How confident are you that you will take this step in the next few weeks?
- What needs to happen for you to take this first step?

Each person takes about seven or eight minutes to discuss their small step. We have used this exercise with considerable success for several years. Some people have a 'light bulb moment' and feel motivated to carry out their small step. Others realise how much of their energy is being invested in exploring the problem. Some are surprised and pleased that they can make progress without doing so!

2 Bringing out the best

The purpose of this exercise is to highlight and reinforce the coachee's resources and effective strategies. This exercise is an adaptation of an exercise by Ben Furman.

- Ask the person about a recent success they have enjoyed. Respond by:

    - Listening.
    - Expressing admiration for their achievement.
    - Ask about some of the difficulties they had to overcome: 'It sounds as if you may have had to . . .'
    - Ask 'How did you do that?'

- Ask 'So how could you use what you have learned from this achievement?'

Practice tips

- Look pleased for the person when listening.
- Communicate genuine admiration but don't go over the top!
- Show curiosity as to how the person achieved what they did.
- Encourage the person to reflect on their success.
- Don't let yourself get in the way, keep your 'coachee' centre stage.

3 Your letter from the future

The author of this exercise is, to the best of our knowledge, Yvonne Dolan. In this version it is being used in a workshop specifically about peoples' work/ life balance.

The facilitator asks members of the group to write the date one year from today at the top of their paper. He invites them to imagine that the intervening year has passed and they are writing to a close friend, family member or colleague. They use this name at the beginning. The coach could say something along the lines of the following.

'When writing the letter from the future, imagine that you are feeling very good about your work (paid or unpaid). You are enjoying what you do, you have a good work/life balance, you are learning a lot and being given the opportunity to use your skills, knowledge and experience. Your level of motivation is high. You feel at your best!

Explain in the letter what has happened over the past year that has enabled you to feel so positive about your life. What is a typical day like for you? Describe your working relationships and activities.

Take ten minutes or so to write the letter, then share as much of it as you wish with one other person in the group. Explore what would need to happen for this imagined future to become reality.'

This can be a powerful exercise that can motivate people towards their goals or help them to realise they are travelling in the wrong direction.

4 Living with change

The coach asks the coachee to relate briefly a story about a time in his/her life when he/she had to cope with a lot of change. The coach simply listens, but encourages with supportive body language. The coach listens for any evidence of the coachee's strengths or skills. The coachee then feeds back what they found the coach did that was helpful and the coach feeds back the strengths and skills the coachee demonstrated.

5 Problem-free talk

Problem-free talk is an integral part of the solution focused approach. This exercise aims to increase the coachee's awareness of their skills and strengths.

The coach/facilitator asks the person about their interests and 'hobbies.' Simply by listening for a few minutes the listener will hear evidence of the coachee's skills and strengths and will be able to reflect them. Where possible the conversation should focus on how these skills and strengths are transferable to areas other than their leisure interests.

Another version of this exercise is to ask the coachee a number of questions such as:

* Would you say you are someone who likes a challenge?
* Do you find it helpful when people tell you what to do?
* Do you like working on your own or do you prefer working with others as a team?
* Do you like to plan things carefully or do you work best when you are spontaneous?

Questions such as these give the coach helpful pointers when it comes to constructing solutions with the coachee. In the exercise the coach would listen and explore the answers and then summarise at the end.

Example

Coach: If I've understood you properly, it's important that we explore your ideas first before I make any suggestions. And that you respond to a challenge as long as it doesn't set you up to fail.

6   Goal stoppers

The coach asks the coachee to think about something she or he does or does not do, which prevents them from achieving a current goal. The coach asks the coachee to describe in more detail what they do/do not do, e.g. 'I talk too much when I'm nervous and trying to impress someone.'

The coach listens without interrupting. After the coachee has said what he wanted to say, the coach asks, 'Why do you think you do this?'

If the answer is self-defeating, e.g. 'I've always done it that way, it's my personality,' the coach sounds doubtful and offers an alternative explanation, one which makes change more possible, e.g. 'I'm not so sure, I wonder if you were more relaxed you would talk less.'

The coach then asks: If you really wanted to change this behaviour how would you sell the change to yourself?

This exercise is loosely based on one used by Bill O'Hanlon.

7 Shoulds, oughts and musts

This exercise highlights the contrast between perceiving behaviour as a duty and seeing it as a free choice. It may look a little strange on paper but it works in practice!

The coachee states something she should or ought to do. The coach responds by simply saying, 'No.' The coachee then restates the behaviour and adds, 'I *could* and I have a choice.'

Coachee: I should tidy my office.
Coach: No.
Coachee: I *could* tidy my office and I have a choice.
Coach: Yes.
Coachee: I ought to phone my brother more often.
Coach: No.
Coachee: I *could* phone my brother more often and I have a choice.
Coach: Yes.

This exercise often leads into a very useful discussion about choice; avoidance; responsibility and power.

8 Find the exceptions

The coach invites the coachee to describe something he does that is problematic, e.g. I put things off/I work too hard/I don't take enough exercise.

The coach listens, making minimal prompts. When the coachee has finished the coach offers a genuine compliment, e.g. 'You've obviously thought about this and want to find a solution that will work for you.'

The coach then asks about exceptions to the problem.

• Are there any times when the problem is not so big, e.g. you get things done/eat better food/take exercise?
• How do these times come about? What do you do to make them happen? Where do you do them? When? With whom?

In the light of these answers the coach asks the coachee to think of one small step they could take to give them a chance of these exceptions happening more often.

9 Four boxes

The coach supports the coachee to complete each box, starting at the top left hand box and working down to the bottom right hand one. This is an amended version of an exercise used by Harry Korman.

Issue	Preferred outcome
Describe the current problem or issue	Describe what the desired outcome would look like
Resources	*Scale*
What personal and social resources does the coachee have that will help them to achieve the preferred outcome?	On a scale of zero to ten, where is the coachee at the moment? If the coachee is higher than zero, how did he or she get there? How could he or she move up one point on the scale?
Any exceptions from which the coachee can learn?	*Next steps*
	What are the next few steps the coachee could take to move forward on this?

10 Scaling walk

Using scales to frame solution focused questions is a key intervention in solution focused coaching. There are many different exercises used by coaches. Some elements of this version come from Paul Jackson and Bill O'Connell.

The coach and the coachee place eleven pieces of paper numbered zero to ten on the floor. They face each other with the row of numbers between them.

The coach asks the coachee about a current goal he has and follows up by asking, 'If ten was that you had already achieved it and zero was that you hadn't started to work on it, where would you place yourself at the moment?'

Whichever number the coachee chooses, both of them walk up to that number. The coach asks, 'How did you manage to get here? What have you done recently that helped you to move up the scale to this point?'

The coach then asks the coachee to face the ten end of the scale and say what it is like to be looking towards that end. Having discussed that the coach then asks, 'Where would you like to get to in the next few days or weeks?' They walk up to that number where the coach asks, 'How would you know that you had arrived here? What would be the first thing that would tell you that you had moved up the scale?'

Returning now to the point on the scale from which they started, the coach asks, 'How could you move up one point on the scale?'

When the coachee answers this question, the exercise ends.

There are of course many other questions associated with scaling such as, 'Has there been a time when you've been higher up the scale?' But with this exercise keeping it clear and simple seems to work best.

11 Motivating yourself

This exercise uses scaling to enable the 'coachee' to gauge their level of commitment to a goal.

Step one

How would you know you had achieved your goal?
What would you start or stop doing that would be different?
What difference would it make to you?

Step two

If ten on the scale means you have already achieved it and zero is you haven't made a start yet, where would you say you are now?

- If above zero, what did you do to get there?
- Where do you hope to get to in the next few days/ weeks?
- What would be one small step that would help you move up one point on the scale?

Step three

If ten is you would put in a lot of effort and zero is you feel unable to do anything, where would you put yourself today?

Is that enough to get you started, or do you need to move up the scale? If you do need to move up the scale what is the first thing you need to do?

Step four

Once the small step has been identified, then ask:

• What would need to happen for that to come about?
• What would you or anyone else need to do?

If the person is not willing/able/ready to take even a small step, ask, 'How will you know when it is a good time to take this step?'

Step five

Summarise what the person has already achieved and what the next step is going to be.

12 Think your way to success

Some elements of this exercise come from Sue Young.

1 The coach asks the person to think of a time when they felt proud about something they had achieved.

• What were you saying to yourself/thinking/hearing from others that helped you to succeed?
• How did you 'psyche' yourself up for the challenge?
• What were you focusing on most – the present moment, past memories, or future benefits?
• How did achieving the goal change the way you think about yourself?
• What did other people notice or say to you about your achievement?

2 The coach then invites the coachee/trainee to think of a time when they 'failed.'

- In the build-up to this experience what were you thinking about/saying to yourself?
- Who were you listening to?
- What were you paying most attention to – past experiences/the present moment/anticipation of the future?
- After the event what did you tell yourself? What did you say to other people and what did they say to you?

The two then discuss the contrast between these two experiences and formulate some 'rules' which enhance the possibility of success for the coachee.

Workshop and group exercises

The following are some examples of exercises suitable for use in workshops and groups.

1 From problems to solutions

This exercise is usually run with three people, with each taking a turn as observer, speaker and coach. The person being interviewed is asked to talk about an issue or concern they currently have.

The first person taking the coaching role interviews the coachee using the problem-focused script below as a frame-work. After five minutes the observer calls time, then the observer re-interviews the coachee about the same issue, using the solution-focused script. A variation on this exercise is to do the solution focused script first.

Problem-focused script

1   Why do you think you have this problem?
2   How do you feel about it?
3   Do you think someone else or the system is to blame?
4   What are the barriers you face?
5   Do you think it is solvable or will you just have to learn to live with it?

Solution-focused script

1 How will you feel when you are managing the situation better?
2 How are you coping with this situation at the moment?
3 Have you had to deal with something similar in the past? What helped?
4 What do you know about yourself that makes you feel that you will get through this problem?
5 What is the next step you could take even if it would not solve the problem completely?

The three then discuss the contrast between the two conversations, e.g. body language/emotional expression/usefulness/positive or negative thoughts and actions.

2 Keeping the future focus

Some groups find this exercise quite challenging, particularly if the coachee's goal is sufficiently vague. It highlights the importance of being precise with language and how we often make assumptions about what others mean. Consequently, we can end up trying to solve problems they don't have!

There can be a certain amount of pressure on people to get three correct answers in a row.

Part one

In groups of five or six, one person volunteers to talk about a goal he or she would like to achieve.

Starting with the person on the 'client's' right he/she asks:

• Do you mean that you . . .?

For example: Person says that their goal is to take better care of themselves.

First Questioner: Do you mean that you need to be more careful about what you eat and drink?

Answer:	Yes.
Second Questioner:	Do you mean that you want to work less?
Answer:	No.

The group needs to get three 'yeses' in a row before continuing to part two.

Part two

The group in turn asks questions to draw out more details of the goal by using some of these below. The questions may come from a list like this:

- What would you be doing/feeling/thinking when you achieve this goal?
- What will other people notice when you achieve this goal?
- What difference will that make to you?
- How does your goal fit with the image you have of yourself?
- If ten is 'everything' and zero is 'nothing,' how much effort are you willing to make to achieve this goal?
- Is that enough and if it isn't what needs to happen?
- If ten is you can absolutely guarantee that you will achieve this goal at some time and zero is that you think it is only a dream, where would you put yourself?
- What will be the first sign that you are making progress in achieving your goal?

Conclusion

'Coachee' states what they got out of the exercise and the group discuss how they managed to keep their focus on the future.

Interview to last 15 minutes and discussion for 15 minutes.

Total 30 minutes.

There is of course no substitute for experiential learning. No matter how well a group coach or trainer may explain or even demonstrate a skill, most people learn best from having a go at it for themselves. Creating a safe learning environment is a key responsibility of the skilled group coach or trainer.

Practice tips

- Be open and flexible during the facilitation of solution focused exercises, observing what is working well and what might be tried differently with this group in the future.
- Consider how individual coaching and workshop exercises you currently use might be adapted for use in a solution focused context.
- Consider how the philosophy and approach of solution focused coaching might help you to deliver your work; what are the different contexts?

Discussion points

- What are the key challenges when coaching with groups and how might these be overcome?
- What is the difference between the role of coach and the role of facilitator?
- To what extent is a solution focused approach likely to be well-received in a commercial business environment?

Recommended reading

Jackson, P.Z. and McKergow, M. (2007) *The Solutions Focus: Making Coaching and Change Simple*. London: Nicholas Brealey International.

Rohrig, P. and Clarke, J. (Eds) (2008) *57 SF Activities for Facilitators and Consultants: Putting Solutions Focus into Action*. Cheltenham: SolutionsBooks.

Final reflections: towards an evidence-based approach

This has been an exciting book to co-author. The three of us bring our own ideas and experiences together to inform the solution focused coaching approach described in this book. In addition, we incorporated the work of others working in the field of solution focused coaching and coaching in general. We have also reflected upon a number of approaches and theories that could inform practice if necessary.

Since 2000 the evidence base for solution focused coaching has been gradually increasing. Among coaching psychologists the surveys over a decade have continued to find that solution focused coaching is a popular approach (Whybrow and Palmer, 2006a,b). This is no real surprise as many practitioners such as Hicks and McCracken (2010) assert that solution focused coaching is already an evidence-based approach and we believe that most coaches and coaching psychologists want to use an effective method. However, for this book we investigated the published research on the solution focused coaching approach. Often it has been integrated with the cognitive behavioural approach, which tends to complicate any research findings. We have concluded that we are currently working towards a sound evidence base for solution focused coaching.

We do hope on a scale of zero to five, where five is really helpful, that you have found this book 'helpful' (three to five on this scale) whether you are a neophyte or experienced personal or executive coach or manager considering intro-ducing a coaching culture or using solution focused coaching skills with staff. The skills, strategies and techniques in this book can be applied to most coaching settings and are relatively straight-forward to apply.

We would appreciate any feedback about this book that you would like to provide us, as we are keen to learn from other practitioners too.

Appendix 1

Solution seeking worksheet

Solution Focused Model

Issue/Problem	Possible solutions and consideration of consequences	Usefulness rating 1–10	Solution implementation steps	Outcome

The *practice solutions* form (adapted © 2009, S. Palmer)

Step 1 Purpose of coaching

What is the purpose of this coaching programme? What is the problem, issue or concern? What would you like to change? Are there exceptions when it is not a problem? How will we know if the situation has improved?

_____

_____

_____

_____

_____

Step 2 Realistic and relevant goals developed

What do you want to achieve? Consider developing SMART Goals, e.g. Select Specific, Measurable, Achievable, Realistic, Timebound goal(s)

_____

_____

_____

_____

_____

Step 3 Alternative solutions generated

What are your options? Write down possible ways of reaching your goals.

_____

_____

_____

_____

_____

Step 4 Consider the consequences

What could happen? How useful is each possible solution? Weigh up the pros and cons. Use a usefulness rating scale: 1–10.

_____

_____

_____

_____

_____

Step 5 Target most feasible solution(s)

Choose the most feasible solution(s).

_____

_____

_____

_____

_____

Step 6 Implementation of chosen solutions

Break down the solution into manageable steps. Now go and do it.

_____

_____

_____

_____

_____

Step 7 Evaluation

How successful was it? Use a rating 'success' scale 1 to 10. Focus on your achievement. What can be learnt? Can we finish coaching now or do you want to address or discuss another issue or concern? Review and revise plan as necessary.

_____

_____

_____

_____

_____

_____

Source material:

Palmer, S. (2007) PRACTICE: A model suitable for coaching, counselling, psychotherapy and stress management. *The Coaching Psychologist, 3*(2): 71–77.

Palmer, S. (2008) The PRACTICE model of coaching: Towards a solution focused approach. *Coaching Psychology International, 1*(1): 4–8.

Palmer, S. (2011) Revisiting the 'P' in the PRACTICE coaching model. *The Coaching Psychologist, 7*(2): 156–158.

Adapted © 2009, Stephen Palmer

References

Alexander, G. and Renshaw, B. (2005) *Super Coaching: The Missing Ingredient for High Performance.* London: Random House Business Books.

Anderson, J.B. (2009) *Mindfulness in Coaching.* Downloaded on 9 July 2011 from http://jbacoaching.com/downloads/MindfulnessCoaching.pdf.

Ashby, W.R. (1956) *An Introduction to Cybernetics.* London: Chapman and Hall.

Association for Coaching (2004) *Summary Report: ROI from Corporate Coaching.* Downloaded on 24 October 2008 from http://www.associationforcoaching.com/memb/ACSumROI.pdf.

Association for Coaching (2005) *AC Competency Framework.* Downloaded on 31 March 2011 from http://www.association-forcoaching.com/about/ACCFrame.pdf.

Association for Coaching (2010) *Code of Ethics and Good Coaching Practice.* Downloaded on 21 June 2011 from http://www.association forcoaching.com/about/about02.htm.

Bachkirova, T., Cox, E. and Clutterbuck, D. (2010) Introduction. In E. Cox, T. Bachkirova and D. Clutterbuck (Eds) *The Complete Handbook of Coaching,* pp.1–20. London: Sage Publications.

Bandura, A. (1986) *Social Foundations of Thought and Action: A Social Cognitive Theory.* Englewood Cliffs, NJ: Prentice Hall.

Bandura, A. (1997) *Self-efficacy: The Exercise of Control.* New York: Freeman.

Beck, A.T. (1976) *Cognitive Therapy and the Emotional Disorders.* New York: New American Library.

Beck, A.T. (1991) Cognitive therapy: A 30-year retrospective. *American Psychologist, 46*: 368–375.

Beck, A.T. and Clark, D.A. (1997) An information processing model of anxiety: Automatic and strategic processes. *Behaviour Research and Therapy, 35*: 49–58.

Belbin, R.M. (1981) *Management Teams: Why They Succeed or Fail.* Oxford: Butterworth-Heinemann.

Belbin, R.M. (1993) *Team Roles at Work.* Oxford: Butterworth-Heinemann.

Berg, I.K. and Szabó, P. (2005) *Brief Coaching for Lasting Solutions.* New York: Norton.

Beyebach, M., Morejon, A.R., Palenzuela, D.L. and Rodriguez-Arias, J.L. (1996) Research on the Process of Solution Focused Brief Therapy. In S. Miller, M. Hubble and B. Duncan (Eds) *Handbook of Solution Focused Brief Therapy.* San Francisco, CA: Jossey-Bass.

Bischof, G. (1993) Solution focused brief therapy and experiential family therapy activities: An integration. *Journal of Systemic Therapies, 12*(3): 61–72.

BPS (2009) *Code of Ethics and Conduct.* Downloaded on 21 June 2011 from http://www.bps.org.uk/sites/default/files/documents/code_of_ethics_and_conduct.pdf.

Bresser, F. and Wilson, C. (2006) What is Coaching? In J. Passmore (Ed.) *Excellence in Coaching: The Industry Guide*, pp.9–25. London: Kogan-Page.

Burke, K. (1969) *A Grammar of Motives.* Berkeley, CA: University of California Press.

Cavanagh, M.J. and Grant, A.M. (2010) The Solution focused Approach to Coaching. In E. Cox, T. Bachkirova and D. Clutterbuck (Eds) *The Complete Handbook of Coaching*, pp.54–67. London: Sage Publications.

Chapman, H. (2006) *Top 10 Tips for Selecting the Right Executive Coach.* Association for Coaching. Downloaded on 13 October 2008 from http://www.associationforcoaching.com/pub/ACSelectingTheRightCoach.pdf.

CIPD (2007) *Annual Learning and Development Survey.* Downloaded on 19 October 2008 from http://www.cipd.co.uk/subjects/lrnanddev/general/_lrngdevsvy.htm?IsSrchRes=1.

Clutterbuck, D. (2007) *Coaching the Team at Work.* London: Nicholas Brealey International.

Collard, P. and Walsh, J. (2008) Sensory awareness mindfulness training in coaching: Accepting life's challenges. *Journal of Rational-Emotive & Cognitive-Behavior Therapy, 26*(1): 30–37.

Cooperrider, D.L. (1986) Appreciative inquiry: Toward a methodology for understanding and enhancing organizational innovation. Unpublished Doctoral Dissertation, Case Western Reserve University, Cleveland, Ohio.

Cooperrider, D.L. and Srivastva, S. (1987) Appreciative Inquiry in Organizational Life. In W. Passmore and R. Woodman (Eds) *Research in Organization Change and Development, 1*: 129–169. Greenwich, CT: JAI Press.

Cooperrider, D.L. and Whitney, D. (1999) A Positive Revolution in Change: Appreciative Inquiry. In D.L. Cooperrider, P.F. Sorensen Jr., D. Whitney and T.F. Yaeger (Eds) *Appreciative Inquiry: Rethinking Human Organization Toward a Positive Theory of Change*, pp.3–27. Champaign, IL: Stipes Publishing.

Cooperrider, D.L. and Whitney, D. (2004) *A Positive Revolution in Change: Appreciative Inquiry*. Downloaded on 8 July 2011 from http://www.tapin.in/images/Appreciative%20Inquiry%20%20Positive%20Revolution%20in%20Change.pdf.

Cortvriend, P., Harris, C. and Alexander, E. (2008) Evaluating the links between leadership development and coaching and performance. *International Coaching Psychology Review, 3*(2): 164–178.

Cox, E., Bachkirova, T. and Clutterbuck, D. (Eds) (2010) *The Complete Handbook of Coaching*. London: Sage Publications.

Csíkszentmihályi, M. (1998) *Finding FLOW: The Psychology of Engagement with Everyday Life*. New York: Basic Books.

de Shazer, S. (1984) The death of resistance. *Family Process, 23*: 30–40.

de Shazer, S. (1988) *Keys to Solutions in Brief Therapy*. New York: W.W. Norton.

Dias, G., Gandos, L., Nardi, A.E. and Palmer, S. (2011) Towards the practice of coaching and coaching psychology in Brazil: The adaptation of the PRACTICE model to the Portuguese language. *Coaching Psychology International, 4*(1): 10–14.

Downey, M. (1999) *Effective Coaching*. London: Orion Business Books.

Drake, D.B. (2007) The art of thinking narratively: Implications for coaching psychology and practice. *Australian Psychologist, 42*(4): 283–294.

Drake, D.B. (2010) Narrative Coaching. In E. Cox, T. Bachkirova and D. Clutterbuck (Eds) *The Complete Handbook of Coaching*, pp.120–131. London: Sage Publications.

Duncan, H. and Miller, S.D. (1999) *The Heroic Client: Doing Client-directed, Outcome-informed Therapy*. San Francisco: Jossey-Bass.

Edgerton, N. and Palmer, S. (2005) SPACE: A psychological model for use within cognitive behavioural coaching, therapy and stress management. *The Coaching Psychologist, 2*(2): 25–31.

Egan, G. (1990) *The Skilled Helper* (4th edition). California: Brooks/Cole.

Ellis, A. (1962) *Reason and Emotion in Psychotherapy*. New York: Lyle Stuart.

Ellis, A. (1994) *Reason and Emotion in Psychotherapy: Revised and Expanded Edition*. New York: Birch Lane Press.

Ellis, A. and Blum, M.L. (1967) Rational training: A new method of facilitating management labour relations. *Psychological Reports, 20*: 1267–1284.

European Mentoring and Coaching Council (2009) *Competency Framework*. Downloaded on 31 March 2011 from http://emccac-creditation.org/wp-content/uploads/2009/10/Competence-Frame work-Oct-20092.pdf.

Freedman, J. and Combs, G. (1996) *Narrative Therapy: The Social Construction of Preferred Realities*. New York: Norton and Co.

Gollwitzer, P.M. (1990) Action Phases and Mind-sets. In E.T. Higgins and R.M. Sorrentino (Eds) *Handbook of Motivation and Cognition 2*, pp.53–92. New York: Guilford Press.

Gonzalez, A.L. (2004) Transforming conversations: Executive coaches and business leaders in dialogical collaboration for growth. *Dissertation Abstract International Section A: Humanities and Social Science*, Vol. 65 (3-A), p.1023. Ann Arbor, MI: Proquest, International Microfilms International.

Gorby, C.B. (1937) Everyone gets a share of the profits. *Factory Management and Maintenance, 95*: 82–83.

Graham, S., Wedman, J.F. and Garvin-Kester, B. (1994) Manager coaching skills: What makes a good coach? *Performance Improvement Quarterly, 7*(2): 81–94.

Grant, A.M. (2001) *Towards a Psychology of Coaching*. Downloaded on 25 April 2011 from http://www.kktf.org/Coaching_review_AMG2001.pdf.

Grant, A.M. (2003) The impact of life coaching on goal attainment, metacognition and mental health. *Social Behaviour and Personality, 31*(3): 253–264.

Grant, A.M. (2006a) Solution focused Coaching. In J. Passmore (Ed.) *Excellence in Coaching: The Industry Guide*, pp.73–90. KoganPage: London.

Grant, A.M. (2006b) Workplace and Executive Coaching: A Bibliography from the Scholarly Business Literature. In D.R. Stober and A.M. Grant (Eds) *Evidence Based Coaching Handbook*, pp.367–388.

Grant, A.M. (2007) Past, Present and Future: The Evolution of Professional Coaching and Coaching Psychology. In S. Palmer and A. Whybrow (Eds) *Handbook of Coaching Psychology: A Guide for Practitioners*, pp.23–39. London: Routledge.

Grant, A.M. (2008) Personal life coaching for coaches-in-training enhances goal attainment, insight and learning. *Coaching: An International Journal of Theory, Research and Practice, 1*(1): 54–70.

Grant, A. and Greene, J. (2001) *Coach Yourself*. Harlow, Pearson Education.

Grant, A. and Palmer, S. (2002) Coaching psychology workshop. Annual Conference of the Division of Counselling Psychology, British Psychological Society, Torquay, UK, 18th May.

Grant, A.M., Curtayne, L. and Burton, G. (2009) Executive coaching enhances goal attainment, resilience and workplace well-being: A randomised controlled study. *Journal of Positive Psychology*, *4*(5), pp.396–407.

Greene, J. and Grant, A.M. (2003) *Solution Focused Coaching*. Harlow: Pearson Education Limited.

Green, L.S., Grant, A.M. and Rynsaardt, J. (2007) Evidence-based life coaching for senior high school students: Building hardiness and hope. *International Coaching Psychology Review, 2*(1): 24–32.

Green, L.S., Oades, L.G. and Grant, A.M. (2006) Cognitive-behavioural, solution focussed life coaching: Enhancing goal striving, well-being, and hope. *Journal of Positive Psychology, 1*(3): 142–149.

Gyllensten, K. and Palmer, S. (2005) The relationship between coaching and work-place stress. *International Journal of Health Promotion and Education, 43*(3): 97–103.

Hausdorff, J.M., Levy, B.R. and Wei, J.Y. (1999) The power of ageism of physical function of older persons: Reversibility of age-related gait changes. *Journal of the American Geriatrics Society, 47*, 1346–1349.

Hawkins, P. and Smith, N. (2006) *Coaching, Mentoring and Organizational Consultancy: Supervision and Development*. Maidenhead: Open University Press.

Hayes, S. C. and Wilson, K. G. (2003) Mindfulness: Method and process. *Clinical Psychology: Science and Practice, 10*(2): 161–165.

Heckhausen, H. and Kuhl, J. (1985) From Wishes to Action: The Dead Ends and Short Cuts on the Long Way to Action. In M. Frese and J. Sabini (Eds) *Goal-directed Behavior: The Concept of Action in Psychology*, pp.134–159. Hillsdale, NJ: Erlbaum.

Hedman, A. (2001) The Person-Centred Approach. In B. Peltier (2001) *The Psychology of Executive Coaching: Theory and Application*, pp.66–80. London: Routledge.

Hicks, R. and McCracken, J. (2010) Solution focused coaching. *PEJ*, January/February, 62–64.

Hoskisson, P. (2003) Solution Focused Groupwork. In B. O'Connell and S. Palmer (Eds) *Handbook of Solution Focused Therapy*, pp.25–37. London: Sage Publications.

Hoyt M. (1995) *Brief Therapy and Managed Care*. San Francisco: Jossey-Bass.

Hutchins, D.E. (1989) Improving the Counselling Relationship. In W. Dryden (Ed) *Key Issues for Counselling in Action*. London: Sage.

International Coaching Federation (2008) *ICF Professional Coaching Core Competencies*. Downloaded on 31 March 2011 from http://www.coachfederation.org/includes/media/docs/CoreComp English.pdf.

Jackson, P.Z. and McKergow, M. (2007) *The Solutions Focus: Making Coaching and Change SIMPLE* (2nd edition). London: Nicholas Brealey Publishing.

Jarvis, J. (2004) *CIPD Coaching and Buying Coaching Services: A Guide*. Downloaded on 19 October 2008 from http://www.cipd.co.uk/subjects/lrnanddev/coachmntor/coachbuyserv.htm.

Jarvis, J. (2005) *The Rise and Rise of Coaching: An Insight into the Increase in Coaching, and how it can Make a Significant Contribution to Business and Play a Major Part in Leadership Development*. Downloaded on 24 October 2008 from http://www.cipd.co.uk/coachingatwork/presales/The+rise+and+fall+of+coaching.htm.

Jeanerod, M. and Prablanc, C. (1983) Visual Control in Movements in Man. In J.E. Desmedt (Ed.) *Motor Control Mechanisms in Health and Disease*. New York: Raven Press.

Johnson, S. (2004) *Mind Wide Open*. New York: Penguin.

Joseph, S. (2010) The Person-centred Approach to Coaching. In E. Cox, T. Bachkirova and D. Clutterbuck (Eds) *The Complete Handbook of Coaching*, pp.68–79. London: Sage Publications.

Joseph, S. and Bryant-Jefferies, R. (2007) Person-centred Coaching Psychology. In S. Palmer and A. Whybrow (Eds) *Handbook of Coaching Psychology: A Guide for Practitioners*, pp.211–228. Hove: Routledge.

Kabat-Zinn, J. (1990) *Full Catastrophe Living: Using the Wisdom of Your Body and Mind to Face Stress, Pain, and Illness*. New York: Delacorte.

Kabat-Zinn, J. (1994) *Wherever You Go, There You Are: Mindfulness Meditation for Everyday Life*. London: Piatkus.

Kampa-Kokesch, S. and Anderson, M. (2001) Executive coaching: a comprehensive review of the literature. *Consulting Psychology Journal: Practice and Research, 53*(4): 205–277.

Katzenbach, J.R. and Smith, D.K. (1993) *The Wisdom of Teams: Creating the High-performance Organization*. Boston: Harvard Business School Press.

Kauffman, C., Boniwell, I. and Silberman, J. (2010) The Positive Psychology Approach to Coaching. In E. Cox, T. Bachkirova and D. Clutterbuck (Eds) *The Complete Handbook of Coaching*, pp.158–171. London: SAGE Publications.

Langer, E.J. (1994) Mindlessness-mindfulness. In R.J. Corsini (Ed.) *Encyclopedia of Psychology*. New York: John Wiley & Sons.

Latham, G.P. and Locke, E.A. (1991) Self-regulation through goal setting. *Organizational Behavior & Human Decision Processes, 50*(2): 212–247.

Lawson D. (1994) Identifying pre-treatment change. *Journal of Counselling and Development, 72*: 244–248.

Lazarus, A.A. (1981) *The Practice of Multimodal Therapy*. New York: McGraw-Hill.

Lazarus, A.A. (1984) *In the Mind's Eye*. New York: Guilford Press.

Lazarus, A.A. (1989) *The Practice of Multimodal Therapy. Systematic, Comprehensive and Effective Psychotherapy*. Baltimore, MD: Johns Hopkins University Press.

Lazarus, A.A. and Abramovitz, A. (2004) A Multimodal behavioural approach to performance anxiety. *JCLP/In Session*, Vol. 60(8), pp.831–840.

Libby, L.K., Shaeffer, E.M., Eibach, R.P. and Slemmer, J.A. (2007) Picture yourself at the polls: Visual perspective in mental imagery affects self-perception and behaviour. *Psychological Science, 18*: 199–203.

Linehan, M.M., Cochran, B.N. and Kehrer, C.A. (2001) Dialectical Behavior Therapy for Borderline Personality Disorder. In D.H. Barlow (Ed.) *Clinical Handbook of Psychological Disorders: A Step-by-Step Treatment Manual*, pp.470–522. New York: Guilford Press.

Linley, A. and Harrington, S. (2007) Integrating Positive Psychology and Coaching Psychology: Shared Assumptions and Aspirations? In S. Palmer and A. Whybrow (Eds) *Handbook of Coaching Psychology: A Guide for Practitioners*, pp.40–56. Hove: Routledge.

Linley, A., Willars, J. and Biswas-Diener, R. (2010) *The Strengths Book: Be Confident, Be Successful and Enjoy Better Relationships by Realising the Best of You*. UK: CAPP Press.

Locke, E.A. and Latham, G.P. (1984) *Goal Setting: A Motivational Technique that Works!* London: Prentice Hall.

Locke, E.A. and Latham, G.P. (1990) *A Theory of Goal Setting and Task Performance*. Englewood Cliffs, NJ: Prentice Hall.

Locke, E.A. and Latham, G.P. (2005) Goal Setting Theory: Theory Building by Induction. In K. Smith and M. Hitt (Eds) *Great Minds in Management*. New York: Oxford University Press.

Locke, E.A., Shaw, K.N., Saari, L.M. and Latham, G.P. (1981) Goal setting and task performance: 1969–1980. *Psychological Bulletin, 90*(1), pp.125–152.

McDonald A. (2007) *Solution Focused Therapy, Theory Research and Practice*. London: Sage.

McDougall, M. (2008) *Association for Coaching: Coaching Supervision: Analysis of Survey Findings*. Downloaded on 19 October 2008 from http://www.associationforcoaching.com/pub/ ACSurveyAnalsysCoachMentorSupervisionJUN08.pdf.

McKergow, M. (2005) Positive Approaches to Organisations and People: Solutions Focus, Appreciative Inquiry and Positive Psychology compared. In M. McKergow and J. Clarke (Eds) *Positive Approaches to Change: Applications of Solutions Focus and Appreciative Inquiry at Work*, pp.1–11. Cheltenham: SolutionsBooks.

McKergow, M. and Clarke, J. (2005) *Positive Approaches to Change: Applications of Solutions Focus and Appreciative Inquiry at Work*. Cheltenham: SolutionsBooks.

McKergow, M. and Clarke, J. (2007) *Solutions Focus Working: 80 Real Life Lessons for Successful Organisational Change*. Cheltenham: SolutionsBooks.

McMahon, G., Palmer, S. and Wilding, C. (2005) *Achieving Excellence in Your Coaching Practice: How to Run a Highly Successful Coaching Business*. London: Routledge.

McNamee, S. (2004) Appreciative Inquiry: Social Construction in Practice. In M. McKergow and J. Clarke (Eds) *Positive Approaches to Change: Applications of Solutions Focus and Appreciative Inquiry at Work*, pp.25–37. Cheltenham: SolutionsBooks.

Miller, W.R. and Rollnick, S. (2002) *Motivational Interviewing: Preparing People for Change* (2nd edition). New York: Guilford Press.

Miller, W.R. and Rollnick, S. (2009) Ten things that Motivational Interviewing is not. *Behavioural and Cognitive Psychotherapy, 37*: 129–140.

Neenan, M. and Dryden, W. (2002) *Life Coaching: A Cognitive Behavioural Perspective*. Hove: Routledge.

Neenan, M. and Palmer, S. (2001) Cognitive behavioural coaching. *Stress News, 13*(3): 15–18.

Norman, H. (2003) Solution focused Reflecting Teams. In B. O'Connell and S. Palmer (Eds) *Handbook of Solution Focused Therapy*. London: Sage.

Nylund, D. and Corsiglia, V. (1994) Becoming solution focused in brief therapy: Remembering something we already know. *Journal of Systemic Therapies, 13*(1): 5–11.

O'Broin, A. and Palmer, S. (2007) Reappraising the Coach-Client Relationship: The Unassuming Change Agent in Coaching. In S. Palmer and A. Whybrow (Eds) *Handbook of Coaching Psychology: A Guide for Practitioners*, pp.295–324. Hove: Routledge.

O'Broin, A. and Palmer, S. (2010) Exploring key aspects in the formation of coaching relationships: Initial indicators from the perspectives of the coachee and the coach. *Coaching: An International Journal of Theory, Research and Practice, 3*(2): 124–143.

O'Connell, B. (1998, 2005) *Solution Focused Therapy*. London: Sage Publications.

O'Connell, B. (2001, 2004) *Solution Focused Stress Counselling*. London: Sage Publications.

O'Connell, B. and Palmer, S. (Eds) (2003) *The Handbook of Solution Focused Therapy*. London: Sage.

O'Connell, B. and Palmer, S. (2007) Solution focused Coaching. In S. Palmer and A. Whybrow (Eds) *Handbook of Coaching Psychology: A For Practitioners*, pp.278–292. Hove: Routledge.

O'Hanlon, B. and Weiner-Davis, M. (2003) *In Search of Solutions*. New York: W.W. Norton.

Palmer, S. (2003) *Multimodal coaching*. Paper presented at The Psychology of Coaching Conference held by the Coaching Psychology Forum at the British Psychological Society's London offices, 15th September.

Palmer, S. (2004) A rational emotive behavioural approach to face-to-face, telephone and internet therapy and coaching: A case study. *The Rational Emotive Behaviour Therapist, 11*(1): 12–22.

Palmer, S. (2007) PRACTICE: A model suitable for coaching, counselling, psychotherapy and stress management. *The Coaching Psychologist*, 3(2): 71–77.

Palmer, S. (2008a) Multimodal coaching and its application to workplace, life and health coaching. *The Coaching Psychologist, 4*(1): 21–29.

Palmer, S. (2008b) The PRACTICE model of coaching: Towards a solution focused approach. *Coaching Psychology International, 1*(1): 4–8.

Palmer, S. (2009) Compassion-focused imagery for use within compassion focused coaching. *Coaching Psychology International, 2*(2): 13.

Palmer, S. (2010) Sports psychology can inform coaching and coaching psychology practice: Internal versus external imagery. *Coaching Psychology International, 3*(2): 15–17.

Palmer, S. (2011a) *Health and well-being coaching: A cognitive behavioural approach*. Keynote paper presented at the Association For Coaching UK Annual Conference on 14th July, 2011 at the University of East London, London, UK.

Palmer, S. (2011b) Revisiting the 'P' in the PRACTICE coaching model. *The Coaching Psychologist, 7*(2): 156–158.

Palmer, S. and Burton, T. (1996) *Dealing with People Problems at Work*. Berkshire: McGraw-Hill Publishing.

Palmer, S. and Cooper, C. (2007, 2010) *How to Deal with Stress*. London: Kogan-Page.

Palmer, S. and McDowall, A. (2010) *The Coaching Relationship: Putting People First*. Hove: Routledge.

Palmer, S. and Panchal, S. (2011) *Developmental Coaching: Life Transitions and Generational Perspectives*. Hove: Routledge.

Palmer, S. and Strickland, L. (1996) *Stress Management: A Quick Guide*. Dunstable: Folens.

Palmer, S. and Szymanska, K. (2007) Cognitive Behavioural Coaching: An Integrative Approach. In S. Palmer and A.

Whybrow (Eds) *Handbook of Coaching Psychology: A Guide for Practitioners*, pp.86–117. Hove: Routledge.

Palmer, S. and Whybrow, A. (Eds) (2007) *Handbook of Coaching Psychology: A Guide for Practitioners*. London: Routledge.

Palmer, S., Grant, A. and O'Connell, B. (2007) Solution focused Coaching: Lost and Found. *Coaching at Work*, 2(4): 22–29.

Passmore, J. (Ed.) (2006) *Excellence in Coaching*. London: Kogan-Page.

Passmore, J. (2011) Motivational interviewing – a model for coaching psychology practice. *The Coaching Psychologist*, 7(1): 36–40.

Passmore, J. and Gibbes, C. (2007) The state if executive coaching research: What does the current literature tell us and what's next for coaching research? *International Coaching Psychology Review*, 2(2): 116–128.

Passmore, J. and Marianetti, O. (2007) The role of mindfulness in coaching. *The Coaching Psychologist*, 3(3), 131–138.

Passmore, J. and Whybrow, A. (2007) Motivational Interviewing: A Specific Approach for Coaching Psychologists. In S. Palmer and A. Whybrow (Eds) *Handbook of Coaching Psychology: A Guide for Practitioners*, pp.160–173. Hove: Routledge.

Peltier, B. (2001) *The Psychology of Executive Coaching: Theory and Application*. London: Routledge.

Pemberton, C. (2006) *Coaching to Solutions*. Oxford: Butterworth-Heinemann.

Peterson, C. and Seligman, M.E.P. (2004) *Character Strengths and Virtues: A Handbook and Classification*. Washington, DC: American Psychological Association.

Prochaska, J.O. and DiClemente, C.C. (1986) Towards a Comprehensive Model of Change. In R.W. Miller and N. Heather (Eds) *Treating Addictive Behaviours*, pp.3–27. London: Plenum Press.

Prochaska, J.O., Di Clemente, C.C. and Norcross, J.C. (1992) In search of how people change. *American Psychologist*, 47: 1102–1114.

Rogers, C.R. (1957) The necessary and sufficient conditions of therapeutic personality change. *Journal of Consulting Psychology*, 21: 95–103.

Rosenkranz, M.A., Busse, W.W., Johnstone, T., Swenson, C.A., Crisafi, G.M., Jackson, M.M., Bosch, J.A., Sheridan, J.F. and Davidson, R.J. (2005) Neural circuitry underlying the interaction between emotion and asthma symptom exacerbation. *Proceedings of the National Academy of Sciences*, 102: 13319–24.

Segal, Z.V., Williams, J.M.G. and Teasdale, J.D. (2002) *Mindfulness-based Cognitive Therapy for Depression*. London: Guildford Press.

Segerstrom, S. (2006) *Breaking Murphy's Law – How Optimists Get What They Want from Life and Pessimists can Too*. New York. Guildford Press.

Seligman, M.E.P. (1999) The president's address. *American Psychologist, 54*: 559–562.

Sharry, J. (2007) *Solution Focused Groupwork* (2nd edition). London: Sage Publications.

Spence, G.B. (2006) *New Directions in the Psychology of Coaching: The Integration of Mindfulness Training into Evidence-Based Coaching Practice*. Downloaded on 9th July 2011 from http://ses.library.usyd.edu.au/bitstream/2123/2469/1/New%20Directions%20in%20the%20Psychology%20of%20Coaching%20(Spence,%202006).pdf.

Spence, G.B. and Grant, A.M. (2007) Professional and peer life coaching and the enhancement of goal striving and well-being: An exploratory study. *Journal of Positive Psychology, 2*(3): 185–194.

Spence, G.B., Cavanagh, M.J. and Grant, A.M. (2008) The integration of mindfulness training and health coaching: An exploratory study. *Coaching: An International Journal of Theory, Research and Practice, 1*(2): 145–163.

Stober, D.R. (2006) Coaching from a Humanistic Perspective. In D.R. Stober and A.M. Grant (Eds) *Evidence Based Coaching Handbook: Putting Best Practices to Work for your Clients*, pp.17–50. Hoboken, NJ: Wiley.

Stober, D.R. and Grant, A.M. (Eds) (2006) *Evidence Based Coaching Handbook: Putting Best Practices to Work for your Clients*. Hoboken, NJ: Wiley.

Stober, D.R. and Grant, A.M. (2006) Toward a contextual approach to coaching models. In D.R. Stober and A.M. Grant (Eds) *Evidence Based Coaching Handbook: Putting Best Practices to Work for your Clients*, pp.355–365. Hoboken, NJ: Wiley.

Stober, D.R., Wildflower, L. and Drake, D. (2006) Evidence-based practice: A potential approach for effective coaching. *International Journal of Evidence Based Coaching and Mentoring, 4*(1): 1–8.

Teasdale, J.D. (2004) Mindfulness-based Cognitive Therapy. In J. Yiend (Ed.) *Cognition, Emotion and Psychopathology: Theoretical, Empirical and Clinical Directions*, pp.270–289. New York: Cambridge University Press.

Thomas, F. (1994) Solution-oriented supervision: the coaxing of expertise. *The Family Journal, 2*(1): 11–17.

UKASFP (2008) *United Kingdom Association for Solution Focused Practice Code of Ethics*. England: UKASFP.

Wasik, B. (1984) *Teaching parents effective problem-solving: A Handbook for professionals*. Unpublished manuscript. Chapel Hill: University of North Carolina.

Watzlawick, P. (1984) *The Invented Reality*. New York: W.W. Norton.

Wesson, K. and Boniwell, I. (2007) Flow theory: Its application to coaching psychology. *International Coaching Psychology Review*, 2(1): 33–43.

Whitmore, J. (2002) *Coaching for Performance*. London: Nicholas Brealey.

Whybrow, A. and Palmer, S. (2006a) Shifting perspectives: One year into the development of the British Psychological Society Special Group in Coaching Psychology in the UK. *International Coaching Psychology Review*, 1(2): 75–85.

Whybrow, A. and Palmer, S. (2006b) Taking stock: A survey of Coaching Psychologists' practices and perspectives. *International Coaching Psychology Review*, 1(1): 56–70.

Wilkins, P. (1993) Person-centred Therapy and the Person-centred approach: a personal view. *Counselling*, 4(1): 31–32.

Williams, H. and Palmer, S. (2009) Coaching in Organizations. In C.L. Cooper, J. Campbell Quick and M.J. Schabracq (Eds) *International Handbook of Work and Health Psychology: Third Edition*, pp.329–352. Chichester: Wiley-Blackwell.

Williams, H. and Palmer, S. (2010) CLARITY: A cognitive behavioural coaching model. *Coaching Psychology International*, 3(2): 5–7.

Williams, H., Edgerton, N. and Palmer, S. (2010) Cognitive Behavioural Coaching. In E. Cox, T. Bachkirova and D. Clutterbuck (Eds) *The Complete Handbook of Coaching*, pp.37–53. London: Sage Publications.

Williams, H., Palmer, S. and O'Connell, B. (2011) Introducing SOLUTION and FOCUS: Two solution focused coaching models. *Coaching Psychology International*, 4(1): 6–9.

Williams, H., Palmer, S. and Wallace, E. (2011) An Integrative Coaching Approach for Family Business. In M. Shams and D.A. Lane (Eds) *Coaching in the Family Owned Business: A Path to Growth*. London: Karnac.

Wilson, C. (2006) *The History of Coaching and the Need for Accreditation*. The Bulletin of the Association for Coaching (8): 7–10. Downloaded on 13 October 2008 from http://www.associationforcoaching.com/pub/ACB0607.pdf.

Yu, N., Collins, C.G., Cavanagh, M., White, K. and Fairbrother, G. (2008) Positive coaching with frontline managers: Enhancing their effectiveness and understanding why. *International Coaching Psychology Review*, 3(2): 110–122.

Web resources and training institutes

adSapiens, Swedish Centre for Work Based Learning
Runs a range of coaching and therapy courses in Gothenburg, Sweden.
www.adsapiens.se

Association for the Quality Development of Solution Focused Consulting and Training
A formal focal point, supporting, promoting and disseminating research and the exchange of knowledge, information, good practice and quality in SF in organisations.
www.asfct.org

Association for Coaching
Association for Coaching is an established professional body. Accredits coaches. Publishes an international journal and AC newsletter.
www.associationforcoaching.com

Association of Coaching Supervisors
The Association of Coaching Supervisors is a professional body with a key mission to actively promote the role of supervision.
www.associationofcoachingsupervisors.com

Association for Professional Executive Coaching and Supervision
Association for Professional Executive Coaching and Supervision is a professional body specialising in executive coaching.
www.apecs.org

Association for Rational Emotive Behavioural Therapy
Professional body that runs conferences, publishes a journal and accredits coaches, therapists, trainers and supervisors.
www.arebt.org

British Psychological Society, Special Group in Coaching Psychology
Professional body focusing on coaching psychology. Publishes two peer reviewed journals, runs events and conferences.
www.sgcp.org.uk

Centre of Applied Positive Psychology
Centre providing training and resources in positive psychology.
www.cappeu.com

Centre for Coaching and Faculty of Coaching Psychology
Based in London, UK. Offers professional-body recognised and university accredited coaching courses at Certificate, Diploma and Post-graduate levels. Specialises in cognitive behavioural and rational coaching.
www.centreforcoaching.com

Centre for Stress Management
Based in London, UK. It runs a Certificate and Diploma programme in Stress Management.
www.managingstress.com

Coaching: An International Journal of Theory, Research and Practice
Coaching is an international, peer-reviewed journal dedicated to the theory, research and practice of coaching. The journal is dedicated to the advancement of coaching research and practice with an international perspective.
www.tandf.co.uk/journals/rcoa

Coaching at Work
Bi-monthly magazine that publishes articles on a range of coaching subjects associated with the workplace. Online resources, coach listing and articles.
www.coaching-at-work.com

Coaching and Mentoring Relationship Research.
This website maintains list of coach–coachee and mentor–mentee publications which are relevant to this book.
www.coachingrelationshipresearch.webs.com

Coaching Psychology Unit, City University London, UK
Undertakes research into coaching, coaching psychology, client-coach/therapist relationship, solution focused coaching, cognitive-behavioural and rational coaching and leadership, stress, health

and wellbeing. It was the first Coaching Psychology Unit to be established in the UK. Offers DPsych and PhD research programmes.
www.city.ac.uk/social-sciences/psychology/research/
coaching-psychology-unit

Coaching Psychology International
Coaching Psychology International publishes short articles on all aspects of coaching psychology, coaching and mentoring. Free access journal.
www.isfcp.net/cpijournal.htm

Focus on Solutions
Company providing solution focused courses and training.
www.focusonsolutions.co.uk

International Academy for Professional Development Ltd
International Academy runs university accredited distance and blended learning courses in coaching and coaching psychology. It is affiliated to the Centre for Coaching. It has a Faculty of Solution Focused Practice.
www.iafpd.com

International Coach Federation
International Coach Federation is a professional coaching body.
www.coachfederation.org

International Society for Coaching Psychology
International Society for Coaching Psychology is a professional body for coaching psychologists. It publishes a journal and has an accreditation scheme for psychologists and recognised courses.
www.isfcp.net/

International Coaching Psychology Review
International Coaching Psychology Review (ICPR) is an international publication focusing on the theory, practice and research in the field of coaching psychology.
www.sgcp.org.uk/sgcp/publications/international-coaching-psychology-review/international-coaching-psychology-review_home.cfm

International Journal of Coaching in Organizations™
The International Journal of Coaching in Organizations™ promotes the sharing of wisdom, insights, theories, models and practices among professional coaches.
www.ijco.info

International Journal of Evidence Based Coaching and Mentoring

The International Journal of Evidence Based Coaching and Mentoring is a free access, international peer reviewed journal.
www.business.brookes.ac.uk/research/areas/coachingandmentoring/?err404=research/areas/coaching&mentoring

Society for Intercultural Education, Training and Research

SIETAR is the world's largest interdisciplinary network for professionals working in the intercultural field.
www.sietar-europa.org

Solution Focused Approaches

Maintains a useful list of solution focused research papers.
www.solutionsdoc.co.uk

The Coaching Psychologist

The Coaching Psychologist (TCP) publishes articles on all aspects of research, theory, practice and case studies in the arena of coaching psychology.
www.sgcp.org.uk/publications/the-coaching-psychologist/the-coaching-psychologist_home.cfm

UK Association for Solution Focused Practice

Professional body for solution focused practice. It holds an annual conference and publishes a journal.
www.ukasfp.co.uk

Index